Email Marketing

Email Marketing Beginners Guide

Email Marketing Strategies

Email Marketing Tips & Tricks

© **Copyright 2016 by Eric J Scott - All rights reserved.**

This document is geared towards providing exact and reliable information in regards to the topic and issue covered. The publication is sold with the idea that publisher is not required to render accounting, officially permitted, or otherwise, qualified services. If advice is necessary, legal or professional, a practiced individual in the profession should be ordered.

- From a Declaration of Principles which was accepted and approved equally by a Committee of the American Bar Association and Committee of Publishers and Associations.

In no way is it legal to reproduce, duplicate, or transmit any part of this document in either electronic means or in printed format. Recording of this publication is strictly prohibited and any storage of this document is not allowed unless with written permission from the publisher. All rights reserved.

The information provided herein is stated to be truthful and consistent, in that any liability, in terms of inattention or otherwise, by any usage or abuse of any policies, processes, or directions contained within is the solitary and utter responsibility of the recipient reader. Under no circumstances will any legal responsibility or blame be held against the publisher for any reparation, damages, or monetary loss due to the information herein, either directly or indirectly.

Respective authors own all copyrights not held by the publisher.

The information herein is offered for informational purposes solely, and is universal as so. The presentation of the information is without contract or any type of guarantee assurance.

The trademarks that are used are without any consent, and the publication of the trademark is without permission or backing by the trademark owner. All trademarks and brands within this book are for clarifying purposes only and are owned by the owners themselves, not affiliated with this document.

Free Gift

As a way of saying thank you for purchasing my book I would like to give you these two books for free.

The first book is ways to improve your copywriting skills to help you write that killer email. The second book gives you 106 amazing ways to build your list.

I think they will both complement this book.

Grab your copy of both of the books.
Visit www.mrmarketinghero.com/freebook

Book To Read

Email Marketing

Beginners Guide to dominating the market with Email Marketing vii

Email Marketing:

Strategies to Capture and Engage Your Audience, While Quickly Building an Authority 77

Email Marketing

Tips and Tricks to Increase Credibility 137

Email Marketing

Beginners Guide to dominating the market with Email Marketing

Table of Contents

Free Gift iii
Book To Read v
Introduction 1
Chapter 1: The Development of Technology 3
Chapter 2: What is Email Marketing? 7
Chapter 3: Why you should use Email Marketing 15
Chapter 4: Pitfalls and How to Avoid Them 23
Chapter 5: How to Start 45
Chapter 6: What to Include in Your Emails 63
Chapter 7: Marketing Concepts 69
Conclusion 75

Introduction

I want to thank you and congratulate you for purchasing the book, *"Email Marketing: Beginners Guide to dominating the market with Email Marketing"*.

This book contains proven steps and strategies on how to effectively begin your journey as an email marketer, how you can steadily advance while developing a strong foundation and how to create more avenues for you to attract more subscribers and ultimately, more wealth.

In addition, I provide you with intriguing background information and statistics so that you can obtain a holistic view of the field you are about to govern. By becoming more knowledgeable about past events, you can have a more in-depth examination on how technology has affected behavioral patterns and market trends.

You do not need to fret that you are just starting. When you are starting something new, you are more open to learning and experimentation. So eagerly embrace and discover as much as you can, as you utilize the various tools and resources that are available. With your new found wisdom and knowledge gained, you can avoid many drawbacks, mistakes and advance even further than individuals who have been in the email marketing field for years. I have included information about the best service providers and programs available, because I sincerely want the best for you.

Email Marketing

This is your time to outshine your competitors and lead in your particular field. Once you make the commitment to employ the various strategies and procedures, you will accomplish your objectives and set goals.

Allow your interest and enthusiasm to fuel your learning drive as I share with you the steps you need to take to obtain the best email marketing results.

Thanks again for purchasing this book, I hope you enjoy it!

Chapter 1

The Development of Technology

It is essential to know when email marketing first came on stream and how it has evolved over the years.

The Advanced Research Projects Agency Network (ARPANET) was the pioneering network that created the technology which is the backbone of what we know today as the internet.

In 1971, Raymond Tomlinson, an American computer programmer, started the first email program on the ARPANET. Prior to Tomlinson's programming, email could only be sent to other users who operated the same computer. He is recognized as the inventor of the email. In 2012, the Internet Society awarded him as an inductee in the Internet Hall of Fame.

Seven years later after Tomlinson started his first email program, Gary Thuerk sent an email promoting Digital Equipment Corp (DEC) machines to 400 users over ARPANET. That was the first time commercial email was sent and it is the first email blast. So if you do not have many subscribers and feel overwhelm when you see companies with 500 000 and 1 million subscribers, do not worry. The first mass emailing was sent to 400 users in 1978. Even if you have 5 subscribers or just 1 subscriber, it is the first step in the right direction.

Gary Thuerk is referred to as "The Father of Spam", as there were complaints by some of the individuals who received his message. It was the first "unsolicited" email blast. On the other hand, Thuerk opined that he views himself as the father of e-marketing as at the time, he concentrated on a targeted list of prospective customers to promote his product.

In 1991, the world was properly introduced to the internet. The European Organization for Nuclear Research known as CERN published a document entitled "New World Wide Web Project". In 1989 at CERN, a British scientist, Tim Berners-Lee had created Hypertext Markup Language (HTML), Hypertext Transfer Protocol (HTTP) and the world's first web pages.

Before, email was only available to workers and students but then personal email addresses were introduced to individuals for free. Hotmail became the first web provider in 1996. Whether an individual had a computer at home or whether they had to use a public computer, anyone could send and receive emails. Email use was no longer restricted to just students and college employees. In 1997, Microsoft bought the company Hotmail for four hundred million dollars.

As other Internet Service Providers (ISP) became available, legislation was updated and enacted in various countries. In the United Kingdom the Data Protection Act was updated in 1998. In the USA the CAN-SPAM Act was introduced and in Europe the Privacy and Electronic Communications Regulations were enacted.

With the influx of emails, ISPs began to filter emails to protect individuals from unwanted communications and viruses. This caused marketers to be more vigilant and to assess data to ensure their emails did not end up in the junk or spam folder.

In 1989, Elwood Edwards voice was recorded for AOL's "You've got mail!" In 1992, the first smartphone became available to individuals. Thus emails could be accessed by mobile. Google was founded in 1998 and in 2007, Gmail became available to the public. In 2004, Facebook was created and more and more social media platforms became available.

Google made Gmail accessible to the public 11 years after Hotmail but today Gmail tops the list as a service provider. Similarly, though you are a beginner, you can dominate the marketing field. All you have to do, is gain as much knowledge as you can and strategically implement what you have learned.

In 2015, there were 900 million Gmail users. The Gmail App has been downloaded more than 1 billion times. Other free Internet Service Providers include Zoho Mail, Yandex, GMX Email, iCloud Mail, Mail.com and Inbox.com.

Chapter 2

What is Email Marketing?

We all communicate with our friends and loved ones via emails. However, besides sending personalized messages to people we already know, we can use emails for other purposes.

Email marketing is utilizing electronic mail to send marketing communication. There are various types of emails which shall be examined.

Welcome Emails

When someone new subscribes to your mailing list, you should send an automated welcome email. It is your first official contact with this subscriber. So let the individual know that you value him or her.

Setting the tone and atmosphere

Furthermore, a welcome email sets the atmosphere for future correspondence. It can be simple and sincere such as, "Welcome to our email list" or "Thank you for signing up to receive our emails". Depending on what your brand is or company offers, you can word it with a bit more flair such as, "Welcome to our group! We are thrilled to have you."

Reinforcement

Always ensure that you fortify the subscriber's decision to sign-up. Let him know that he made a wonderful decision by filling in his information to receive emails from you. You can explain what he is expected to receive now, that he has joined your list. Examples can include:

- Access to other parts of your website reserved for subscribers only
- Specialized information
- Notification about special events

Present a deal

You have the option of offering a valued deal such as a discount or a gift. Let's imagine for a minute that you visit a new store that has just opened. Your intention is to browse the shelves and see what they have to offer. On entering the store, you are a given a complimentary treat and before you can even look in the showcase glass, you are given a discount voucher. Won't you feel extra special? Sure you will. That type of treatment will cause you to speak well of the store and even tell your friends about it.

Likewise, imagine how your new subscriber will feel when you offer something of value. He will surely feel extra special. You do not have to overextend yourself financially, but there are bits of information and deals you can offer. You just have to be creative about it.

Call to Action

A call to action (CTA) in marketing, means a directive that you give to someone to perform an action. In your welcome communication, ensure that you have a call to action. You can have a notification to "download" information or "shop now" or "browse our store". If you do not have a store, you can indicate to the subscriber what you will like him to do.

Feature your service or product

Do not lose sight of your objective. Remember you are marketing. It is acceptable to have images promoting your brand, product or service. Use emotive images for persuasion.

Be mindful of mobile users

Ensure that whatever platform you use, that the welcome email is also mobile friendly. Many individuals check their emails on their mobile phones. Make sure the script is clear and the images are visible. This is your first opportunity to impress your subscribers, so make sure that you do a great job.

Include social media buttons

Your subscribers wish to know more about you. Feed their curiosity by including your social media platforms in your welcome letter. This is a great way to allow your subscribers to keep in touch with you.

Informative Emails

Everyone likes to be kept informed. These type of emails educate your subscribers on a particular topic. You can give the solution to challenges or answer certain queries. You can also inform your subscriber about what is new on your website or what is happening in your company.

When writing informative emails, remember that not everyone is detail oriented. Yes, they would like the information but lengthy emails can be a turn-off for some people. This is what you can do:

Place the key detail(s) early

By doing this, if someone does not have time to read your email at the moment, the main point will be conveyed nonetheless.

If you have many details in your email, then you can have an opening summary. That way the readers can read on if they want more details. If they don't read on, you still conveyed your message in the summary. Once what you have outlined is engaging, when the reader has more time, he will read your email to the end.

Use bold, underline or italics to highlight

This will cause your subscriber to pay more attention to what you have highlighted. This can include the date or location of an event. Avoid using peculiar and oversized fonts.

Use bullet points and lists

Rather than have long-winding paragraphs, you can use bullet points. There are rules pertaining to bullet points. Ensure that you observe them so that the appearance of your email looks tidy.

Refrain from using multi-level bullet points or lists. Ensure that your numbering is consistent. Look at this example below. There are various tiers of lists and the numbering is inconsistent.

1) Eggs
   a) Cheese
   b) Bacon
      i) Milk
      ii) Bread
         (1) Fruit
         (2) Yogurt

You may think that this is very basic and no way will you ever make the mistake. However, realize that even when you do things correctly, your numbering may be inconsistent. Without testing how your email will appear on various devices, and based on your email settings, sometimes what may look good in your template may be askew in someone else's inbox. That is why it is very important to preview your emails on a computer and on mobile devices before emailing them.

Differentiate when it is best to use bullet points and numbering. When mentioning steps, for example, it is better to use numbering. For example, you may write on the topic "Steps to Boost Your Confidence". Out of habit, you may use 15 bullet points. Then you may mention that Steps 7 and 9 were difficult for you to implement. What you have done is, you used up the reader's valuable time by having him or her count the bullet points to figure out which one is Step 7. If you had numbered them, it would have been easier to see which steps you are referring to.

Use subheadings correctly. Also, keep uniform styles. Do not use a full sentence in your bullet points or list and then switch to listing items and then use a fragment of a sentence. Again, the appearance of your email is very important.

Using the same example above, let us assume your topic is about the nutrition in the foods we consume for breakfast. This is what I am referring to:

- Eggs contain protein and Vitamin D which is great for our bones.
- Cheese
- Bacon – source of animal protein

The styles used in our example are different. There is a full sentence in the first point. The next point is itemized and no nutritional value is given and then in the last point, a fragment is used. Whatever you do, be consistent throughout. Additionally, ensure that what you have promised is delivered. If you inform your readers you will do something or provide information, remember to back check to make sure that you have not forgotten.

Status Order Emails

Subscribers should be kept updated about whatever they ordered and if something is to be shipped, the progress of the shipment, delivery, and receipts. These types of emails are known as transactional emails. These emails are a way to foster a good shopping experience for your subscriber.

Abandonment Shopping-Cart Emails

These are notices to inform your subscribers that they did not conclude the purchase. This is a way to persuade subscribers to follow through with the purchasing transaction. It is essential that you utilize these emails as you will be neglecting opportunities to earn revenue.

Reorder Emails

These are notifications you will send to subscribers reminding them to repurchase your service or product. Be creative in your approach. Yes, you wish to earn more revenue but do not harass your subscribers by sending many of them.

Reengagement Emails

As time goes by, some subscribers would not be as actively engaged as others. From analyzing your data reports, you may observe that some of your subscribers haven't opened or clicked on your email for a long time. We will examine more about data reports. It is necessary to send emails to know who are your active users.

Holidays/Birthdays/Anniversaries

You can have a section of your form where subscribers can fill in their date of birth. This way, on their birthdays, you can let them know how much you appreciate them by sending a greeting. Moreover, you can alert them as to special offers and discounts and even send coupons in these emails. This is an opportune time to boost your sales and peak your customers interest in your product.

You can also send discount and offers for the various holidays and your company's anniversary and milestones.

Newsletters

These are emails sent on a regular schedule. For example weekly or monthly. However often you decide to send them, they serve many objectives. They foster brand loyalty, ensure that you stay in touch with your subscribers and is a viable way to attract new prospects.

Digest Emails

This is a shortened version of a newsletter consisting mainly of lists and links.

Sales Announcement Emails

As the title signifies, these emails are sent when you have something to announce about your product or service to garner more interest in what you offer.

Recommendation Emails

You may see this sometimes worded as "cross-sell" emails. First, you monitor what your customers have bought and then you send emails recommending other products and services the subscriber may like. For example, if you sell beauty products and several of your subscribers purchase a particular skin cream, you may let them know about similar products which they may like.

Events Email

If you are having an event, you will send emails informing your subscribers about the events whether they be a product launch, presentations, seminars, webinars or conferences. After sending your initial invitation, you will have to send a follow-up and reminders. After the event, you should send thank-you correspondence.

Website Trigger Emails

As a subscriber spends time on your website, you can collect data on where they clicked on your website. Then send applicable emails to subscribers with pertinent information.

Lead Nurturing Emails

Lead nurturing is a marketing term which refers to developing relationships with prospective clients. If someone is looking at what you have to offer and even if they are not, lead nurturing makes your business more visible so that when a customer is ready to purchase, your company will be the first option.

Once you have your subscriber's information, you can communicate by sending emails about your products or services, changes in the cost or any updates that will influence the client to favorably view your products and services.

Lead nurturing is a traditional way of marketing but it has evolved since the development of so many social media platforms.

Chapter 3

Why you should use Email Marketing

Centuries ago, traveling by horse was one of the methods used to convey messages on land. If the person was overseas, boats and ships were the only medium to deliver correspondence. Today, email is the strongest resource to send messages. Not only can you communicate using email, but you can obtain valuable data. How is it done? It is done by installing an email tracking app in your email. When you use the tool, you will be notified about your tracked emails. You will receive notifications as to who opened them, what was clicked and viewed and the time.

What about social media?

Comparison

Facebook

Statistics from Statista, a data portal, reveal that as of the first quarter of 2016, there were 1.65 billion users who were actively engaged in this platform on a monthly basis. In order words, the number of people who signed into their account within 30 days was 1.65 billion. It is by far the most popular social media platform.

Twitter

By the end of 2015, sources reveal that active monthly users for Twitter were 305 million. By the first quarter of 2016, there were 310 million active users. Note that this is active users. These are quite impressive numbers.

Email users

When you combine Facebook and Twitter account, they are still more active *email* users. Statistics from Radicati Group, reveal that in 2015, there were an estimated 2.5 billion email users. This proves that email marketing is a very powerful resource. The figure for daily emails sent and received in 2015 was 205 billion! The average business emails sent and received per person is 122 emails daily.

Subscribers see your email messages

Moreover, Facebook and Twitter still use email to alert users of activity or about their pages. You must take into consideration also that when you post things on Facebook, not all your fans will see what you posted. Even if you keep posting it, there is a limitation to the times it is featured in its news feed. Remember that Facebook has paid advertising options and prefer if people pay for their advertising than posting in their newsfeed, hence the limitation. Businesses are subjected to changes and the regulated newsfeed of Facebook.

Your subscribers actively signed up to be a part of your mailing list. Therefore when you send emails, they will be expecting to hear from you, not tag your emails as spam. When you email to your subscribers, there is no limitation to who will see you messages. Therefore your email is more effective, as it reaches your targeted audience. When you send an email, to your subscriber's inbox, you are not at the mercy of any social media platform policy.

Conversions

Studies reveal that more subscribers click more on the information you have sent in your emails than the average clicks from a tweet. More people will click on the information in your email that links them to your website or blog more times, than other social media.

Emails are not controlled by big companies limiting you to what you send and receive from your subscribers.

Long standing

Every day, social platforms vie to increase their ranking. Some social platforms that existed ten years ago are not even in the top ten popular social media today. On the other hand, email users have been growing consistently throughout the years. It is best to invest your time and resources in something that is long lasting and that is email marketing.

Most Popular Websites Globally and What Can Be Learnt

If you wish to dominate the market, note the services the giants in the industry are offering. Also observe the strategies these companies have implemented to obtain ideas and ways to improve your marketing strategy.

Google

Globally, search engine www.google.com is the top-ranking website. Besides the search engine, Google offers advertising programs, web browser Google Chrome, Gmail and YouTube.

If you wish to drive traffic to your site, have valuable information and knowledge that other people wish to obtain. You can have links and let people know about other resources available that they may be interested in.

Facebook

Facebook was formed by fellow students in 2004. Today it is the 2nd most highly ranked website.

You can integrate Facebook and email marketing by implementing these strategies. In your emails include the Facebook icon so your users can follow you. You can provide sign-ups on your Facebook page. Host competitions on Facebook. There are many apps available to assist you with your objectives.

If you have a brand or small business, and you know of other people who share the same vision, team up or form partnerships to advance your business growth. If you are a blogger for example, you can be a guest blogger on your associate's blog and market to a new audience. Or your friend or associate can ask subscribers to his or her mailing list, whether they will will be interested in receiving emails from you. They can also share what you post on your Facebook page on their page too.

YouTube

Originally, YouTube was created in 2005, by three individuals who once worked at PayPal. Google acquired it in 2006. The days of reading through boring documents to gain knowledge are over. With videos on every topic, many people around the world visit YouTube to view what others have to share as well as upload their own content.

You can share informative videos with your subscribers. Share with them what you have learned and invite them to share their opinions. On a daily basis, almost 5 billion videos are viewed. Your subscribers want to hear from you and obtain information too. Therefore integrate this platform into your email marketing strategy.

Yahoo

Yahoo was officially established in 1995 and services include Yahoo Search, Yahoo Mail, Yahoo Finance, Yahoo News and Yahoo Answers. Depending on what type of business you have, or if you blog, you can comment about the popular topics in the news.

Amazon

Amazon is a popular e-commerce site that was established in 1994. What lessons can you learn from Amazon? Have you ever bought something on Amazon and there are other products which are recommended based on your recent purchase? Your information as to what you bought and when it was shipped is meticulously recorded. They are masters at tracking and recording. As an email marketer, you must understand the importance of tracking what your customers do.

Also, if someone abandons your shopping cart, ensure that you follow up by sending an email.

Look at the design of Amazon. The company's website and email designs are consistent. They are good at branding using a simple design.

Wikipedia

Wikipedia is an online encyclopedia that was founded in 2001. It is the 6th most popular website in the United States and 7th in the world. You may wonder, how can I use Wikipedia for my email marketing strategy? This is how.

Create a Wikipedia Page

For a page to be created, the topic must be "notable" according to Wikipedia's guideline. If the topic is newsworthy and you have trustworthy sources you can qualify. The online source has all the guidelines on what you need to know and do. You will have to monitor your page if you do take this route for anyone can add to it. When you sign up for your account change the setting so you can be notified when a change to your page occurs. You can also opt-in to exchange emails with other Wikipedia users. There is also something known as "talk page" where you can communicate with other users. It is one way to build credibility and promote your brand.

Twitter

Twitter is a social media platform that was launched in 2006. It is one of the most popular social media and you should integrate Twitter in your email marketing plan. You can upload your subscriber list to your Twitter network. It enables you to build your Twitter community and gain new followers.

Additionally, you can follow your subscribers to observe what interests they have and to give you a better understanding on how best to market your products and services to them. It also strengthens relationships.

You can synchronize your Twitter account to your email account to scan your contacts. On Twitter's website twitter.com, on the sidebar, there is a link that conveys that you can search to locate people you know. Twitter will check your emails with what is in the company's database.

Moreover, you can use Twitter ads to target a section of your group when you have promotions and offers. If you wish to promote your communication on Twitter, visit the Twitter advertising section and sign in. If you are new to Twitter, you will have to enter more information. Then you will answer queries about your promoted tweet campaign. You have the option to select your targeted users on the basis of keywords or a television show for example. Or you can focus your promotion to individuals in a particular location or gender. The next step is to set your budget and add your payment method. There are other ways in which you can promote your brand. Visit the website and look at what services are available.

To increase your Twitter followers, pay attention to your profile. What profile picture are you using? If you do not have an account as yet, which picture will you use? Make sure that you are using a picture of yourself. You can have more than one Twitter account. So create a business Twitter account if necessary where you can use the business logo and promote your brand.

Ensure the picture you are using is large enough. If your image is blurry it gives a poor reflection of you, or your brand if you are using your business logo. Use hashtags, which are specific keywords used to increase your rankings. Do not use too many hashtags and avoid using very long ones. Use them properly.

Additionally, you can use the "Click to Tweet" generator. Individuals who want to share your information but find it a bit tedious to type information about your offer or service, can simply share your tweet. It is sometimes referred to as a lazy tweet as individuals simply share what you have already typed in the tweet.

It is a very effective tool to promote your brand and product. Include links for individuals to use on your blog, email and website. What is great about it, is that you get your message shared the exact way you wish the information to be shared. You do not want anyone misunderstanding your correspondence or interpreting what you have expressed incorrectly.

Chapter 4

Pitfalls and How to Avoid Them

As a beginner, you have much information at your disposal. You can assess various reports, read testimonials, observe the challenges many people face and plan your strategy. You do not have to repeat the mistakes of others. You will be knowledgeable on what you should avoid so that when you start your campaign you dominate the market.

The best time to climb your mountaintop is now. Let us examine the various factors that can hinder your growth. Therefore ensure that you pay keen attention to these details.

Ensure your subject line is reflective of the content

There is nothing wrong with getting excited. You would like subscribers to open your emails in anticipation. You would like them to click your links that will lead them to your website. However, with all your frenzied anticipation you should maintain your integrity and not disappoint your subscribers.

You may wonder, "In what way can I possibly disappoint my subscribers in my subject line?" Have you ever eaten at a restaurant and the waiter tells you about a mouth-watering entrée that customers have given rave reviews. You abandon what you had planned to order in anticipation for the recommended cuisine. When you finally taste it, you think that they have surely given you the wrong meal. You're not sure if to argue or to immediately leave.

Similarly, you disappoint your subscribers when your subject line lures your subscribers to open your email, but the content is completely different. Your subject lines may inform them of a topic that is so thrilling and something they want to know so much more about, yet when they open the email, the topic is not mentioned again. Or if it is, it is a watered down version of what you said. Your subscribers are no longer optimistic. Instead, they are deflated and quite frankly they feel like you set them up, you've misled them. Guess what, next time you send an email they will be very suspicious about opening it. It may even be deleted forthwith.

You may trick them temporarily but the long-term impact is much more detrimental as your subscribers will grow to mistrust you. Therefore, if you mention something in the subject field, ensure that you elaborate about the topic more in your content.

Preheader

Another mistake is that the preheader is ignored. Next to the subject line, the text that can be seen is referred to as the pre-header. These are the few words that make up the first line in your email. Some platforms vary.

The body of the email is important and the subject line, but the preheader should not be overlooked as it is an opportunity to allow your personality to shine through.

The reply to is unknown

Has someone ever left a message for you and on reading the note, the message is very important. This correspondence is so urgent that you need to contact the sender, only to have the individual who gave you the note inform you that she didn't write down the person's name. She forgot to write down that vital piece of information. You wish and hope that the person would fax, email, call or visit you in person. To your disappointment, days pass and the person is still not identified.

It is the same way, when you send emails and the subscriber looks to reply for whatever reason, he sees "no reply". It can be very off-putting. In the example above, the person was not able to be contacted because the person who received the message forgot to write the name down. In this example however, by using "no reply" you do not wish to be contacted.

Or even if you have a reply address, but you do not check that email address, it is like the address doesn't exist either. It is like every time someone calls you, your answering machine cuts in and no matter how many messages are left, you still do not return the call.

The purpose of emails is to stay in touch with your subscribers and engage with them. Do not send the wrong signals that you do not wish to communicate with them or if you do, it is only on your terms.

Do not send dull and unfriendly emails

Sometimes marketers send emails that have nothing of use or significance to the subscriber. It is not only about sending emails with the words in caps: BUY NOW! You know the value of your product and service. Yes you want many people to purchase what you have to offer but the foundation must be set that your subscribers know that when they open your email, it entails something that has merit.

Do not judge the value of your email just on how quickly someone pays for your product or service. Once you have something that is worthy, you will eventually see the dollars. It is all about building a valuable relationship over a period of time. Your subscribers will eventually tell others about your brand.

Focus more on how your service or product can serve your subscribers more than focus on your product or service *only*. You have to make the connection and let them know how they will benefit from using it.

There are too many calls to action

A call to action (CTA) is a directive that you give to your subscribers to elicit an instant response. You can have a button on your website that says: "Request a Demo" or "Click for a Free Trial".

Netflix for example instructs subscribers to, "Join Free for a Month" as well as the promise that you can "Cancel Anytime".

An email is not like a job application. In a job application, you list all your top attributes and credentials and everything you wish to influence a company to call you for an interview and ultimately hire you. You do not have a chance to send a follow-up job application where you highlight other things you did not include in the first job application.

With an email, you can send more than one and give information accordingly. Therefore, do not add too many calls to action. Let's imagine for a moment if you receive an email and on opening it, there are 12 calls to action buttons with different neon colors, all conveying a different directive. Won't you feel overwhelmed?

To avoid this, focus on what you wish to communicate with your readers in that specific email and then design your email accordingly with the appropriate buttons, links or forms for them to visit your page.

Failure to provide a link

Place a link where it is visible to your subscribers without them having to scroll down. The terminology is referred to as place a link "above the fold." Also, place a link "below the fold" which means that you will have to scroll down to view it.

Lengthy Emails

For some marketers, there is the notion that long emails mean that you are giving your subscribers more value. Thus emails are filled with various topics and news. However, it takes the subscriber a very long time to read them and digest what you wish to convey.

You can send several shorter emails or use bullet points to condense your message.

Know how to use images

Images should enhance your emails, not be used only as the content of your email. Remember that some subscribers check their emails from their phones. If images do not load properly on their mobile phones they will not be aware of what your wish to communicate in your email.

Additionally, some subscribers have their setting adjusted that images are blocked.

Also, you can use at least an image in your email. Ensure that the option of using plain text is utilized also.

Be consistent with your emails

Your subscribers expect to hear from you. Do not have a steady flow of emails and then cease to email for a couple of months and then start again. There must be the right balance. Do not get too enthusiastic and send too many emails for this can be as annoying as someone who calls your phone too many times.

Have a regular schedule. You can start by sending one every two weeks. If you are not sure how many emails to send out, you can have an option that allows subscribers to select how frequently they wish to receive emails. Thereafter you can segment your subscribers and send emails according to their preferences.

Failure to send emails

When you have collected emails, you do not need to wait until you have something major to share with your audience to send emails. You can nurture your subscribers in the meantime. This doesn't mean that you should send pointless and baseless emails just for the sake of keeping in touch. If you have a major event four months away, you can send nurturing emails, even if it is a minimum of once per month. That way when you do send emails about your huge event, you have already nurtured them and created a foundational framework with which to share your major event. Your subscribers will forget who you are and may wonder, "Who is this again? Why am I receiving messages?" Stay in touch.

Manage your email list

You need to monitor which subscribers do not open your emails. Constantly emailing these non-responsive subscribers can cause your emails to end up in the spam folder on the presumption that it is junk email you are sending.

Monitor and once you have identified your subscribers who do not open your emails at all over a long period of time, stop sending emails to them.

Segment your Email List

Depending on what you offer, it is very important to assess and segment your list. For example, let us say that you offer courses on your website, and you have beginners and advanced subscribers, you won't send the same information that you send to your beginners to your advanced users.

You can also do surveys to get to know your subscribers better and ascertain what other information you can also impart to them. This adds a personable touch.

The Importance of Tracking and Segmentation

Tracking

Technology has developed to such an extent that gone are the days when an email is sent and we remain hopeful that it was delivered and opened by the receiver.

Today, there is software that enables us to know when a person opens our emails, click on the links provided and view the attachments. There is no interruption to our busy lives as everything is done in the background.

An image pixel that is invisible, is placed in your emails that inform about the date, the time the email was opened and the device used by the recipient. There is no invasion of anyone's privacy. The software informs you about the data relating to your particular email, not about what is happening in your subscriber's inbox.

Tracking enables you to use your time more efficiently. You can assess when your emails were opened rather than sending out emails again inquiring, "Did anyone receive my emails?" Or sending them out a second time. If you also note that a section of your audience opened their mail at a specific time, it gives you an idea of when to send the other emails.

Moreover, if you wish to follow up with a phone call to one of your business contacts or subscriber you will know when it is the best time to call.

Assessing your data can also highlight other things, such as unsubscribes and bounced email rate. Bounced emails is a marketing term to describe when your emails could not be delivered. There are hard and soft bounces. Hard bounces mean that the addresses were denied. Possible reasons for this is that the address is no longer active or the domain name does not exist. Soft bounces refer to addresses that have a temporary issue. It could be that your recipient's inbox is full or the server may be temporarily inoperative.

Some marketing systems cannot track plain text emails and some do. So be mindful of this when choosing an email service provider. Email tracking also allows you obtain other information about your subscribers such as their social profile.

Segmentation

One very important marketing strategy that is ignored is segmentation. It means to divide your email lists so that you send your subscribers and customers the correct email at the right time. For example, if you sell men and ladies footwear, you should not send certain information pertaining to female shoes to your male audience.

Firstly, you should differentiate your emails. When individuals sign up, you can have the gender on your forms so they can select accordingly. You can also differentiate as to location or age group. What is your business about? What do you do? Think of the various headings where segmenting your list can benefit you.

Keep your goal in mind and develop a strategy to meet that goal. For example, you may want more people to know how valuable your products are. When you sell your products, you can ask your purchasers to review it. That way more people will know what other people have to say. Segmentation allows you to know your subscribers much better.

To recap, these are what you should observe.

Pay attention to the subject line and your preheader. Have a reply to address. Do not have a noreply@xcompany.com. Take cognizant of the fact that you are not meeting your subscribers face to face. It is not a business meeting or luncheon where you and your subscribers have time to know more about each other's character and personality. Therefore your email must convey all that you would like them to know about you. You are not a robot, devoid of human personality. You can still maintain your professionalism and be relaxed and engaging. Your subscribers want to know more about you and the advantages of purchasing your product or service so do so in an engaging tone.

Moreover, make your call to action or calls to action well defined and specific. Do not place too many in an email. Place links appropriately. Your emails should be short, informative and engaging.

Always ensure that you have text in your emails and be consistent with keeping in touch. Segment and manage your list by frequently assessing your data.

Email Service Providers

Perhaps you are feeling overwhelmed and you are a bit baffled by the specifics of tracking emails. You may have seen the letters ESP and may have wondered what it means. In the world of email marketing, ESP does not refer to extrasensory perception. You do not have to be telepathic to be a great marketer. ESP is the abbreviation for Email Service Provider.

I have assisted you by listing some of the leaders in the industry. There are many more service providers and they are just as reputable. However, I have listed the popular ones so you can compare the others to them and make your choice. Your Email

Service Provider will have the necessary resources for you to become more effective as an email marketer.

Note that I have highlighted only some of the benefits and limitations. The topics are highlighted for you to make the observation and not overlook certain issues.

iContact

The company was founded in 2003 and it is located in North Carolina, USA. The website is www.icontact.com.

iContact in its guide, outlines some features that customers will obtain without having to pay extra for it. This includes uncomplicated sign-up forms and autoresponders; email deliverability; great templates, data that allows you to know more about your customers; technical support; a platform that combines social network with email campaigns and analytical reporting. The company constantly updates its tools and resources to keep ahead of its competitors. In addition, the company allows subscribers to a free 30-day trial. If you like iContact's service, you can then pay monthly.

You do not have to be knowledgeable about HTML coding to use them. Since 2008, iContact has received many awards. In 2010 they were the awarded the #1 spot as the Email Marketing Provider in a pool of 50 companies by website magazine. Top Ten Reviews ranked them as #1 in their 2015 and 2016 compilation. The company is included in Capterra's Top 20 and G2 Crowd highly ranked the company Best of Breed Leader for Summer 2015 and Winter 2016.

The basic plan ranges from US$14 to US$117 depending on a number of your subscribers. The Pro Pricing ranges from US$99 to US$249. The Pro Package functions with Google Analytics, has advanced options and you will be assigned an advisor. There is also a Premier Package.

Benefits

iContact is one of the leading email service provider.

The company provides uncomplicated tools and a range of features and reports.

Limitations

You will not be supplied with Google Analytics in your basic plan. Note however that the company has an excellent reporting so you will still be able to track your data. There is an iContact App which allows you to track your data, add contacts and preview emails for example.

There is a limited autoresponder.

Your image storage is only 5 MB. To counter this, you can buy more storage space

Live chat and telephone support are not available on weekends. To counter this, the website provides customers with tutorials, webinars, a blog, and guides.

Some former customers have expressed that they encountered some hassles while trying to cancel their account.

Benchmark

Benchmark is located in California and was founded in 2004. The website is www.benchmarkemail.com.

The metrics are simple and will be good for new marketers learning the industry. As you get more advanced, you should note how this may affect you. There are free plans where you do not have to give your credit card information. Note however that on your emails will be the company's logo for the free plan.

There is a 30-day trial that ends after the time or if you send a low quota of emails. There are the company's forms you can use for free signup on your website or Facebook page.

For the basic plan, there are three various pricing. You can purchase storage if you need more space. You can import a list if you have one. The company has a quick reporting system compared to others. You can track your open rates and unsubscribes pretty easily. There is the ability to export the data.

Benefits

Email, Telephone and Live Chat Support are available. On Saturdays, for a few hours, you will obtain email and live support. This is a plus as most companies do not offer support on weekends.

Limitations

It relies on Google Analytics for conversion tracking. It is ideal for a new marketer but as you advance you may need more data than the company provides.

Information is sometimes hard to locate. For example, information about the free for life branding on your email was found in the Frequently Asked Questions page and not on the Free For Life page. Therefore, you have to read many articles to get a gist of what you will obtain as it is not as organized as many customers would have liked. Also, it is best to confirm with the support department that what you have read, is accurate as some of the Frequently Asked Questions information may not be current. There are videos, manuals, articles and tutorials available to guide you.

Pinpointe

The company was founded in 2008 and it is located in California. The website is www.pinpointe.com.

The price ranges from $49 per month to $898 depending on your number of subscribers. Subscribers range from 5000 contacts to over 200 000. You also have the option to pay-as-you-go where you pay per email that is sent with an unlimited number of contacts. The price for pay-as-you-go ranges from 25 000 emails at $245 to 1 million emails for $2850 If you only have a few contacts and will send out an occasional newsletter, it is best to use another ESP. Pinpointe is designed to handle heavy traffic. There is a 15-day free trial.

Benefits

Interface is easy to use.

You can use Google Analytics.

The company gives suggestions on how to fix your emails to ensure that they will be viewed properly.

Autoresponders and surveys are available.

Tracking and Reporting are available.

Marketers express that the customer support is very good. They have telephone chat, live chat, and email support.

Limitations

You may spend more time learning Pinpointe than some of the other ESPs.

As with many other providers, technical support not available on weekends. You can counter this by viewing the videos that are available on the site and YouTube.

Customers have conveyed that there is a limited range of templates.

GetResponse

This company was established in 1999 in Poland and operated exclusively in Europe. Today it has offices also in the USA and Canada with users in almost 200 countries. The website is www.getresponse.com. The company has received many awards and in 2013 was given a Blue Ribbon Award by the USA Chamber of Commerce. The company has also received bronze, gold and silver awards for customer service training and video tutorials.

There is a 30 day free trial for up to 250 subscribers. The basic plan is $15 monthly for up to 1000 subscribers and up to $450 per month for up to 100 000 subscribers. There are Pro and Max packages which give you admission to the company's webinars.

Benefits

There is a 1 GB image storage. Users have access to over 1000 images in the company's library.

There is great reporting, from basic to advanced reports.

Chat support is available all the time, which is an added bonus if you have challenges, especially on weekends. You can also contact support through an online form and there is a phone support on weekdays.

There are many video tutorials, materials, articles and blogs which can be downloaded and you can have access to live webinars.

Limitations

Advanced email marketing tools may cause you to feel overwhelmed as a new timer. However, you can contact their support teams to assist you.

There are organized templates which are arranged in categories.

Constant Contact

The company officially started operation in 1998 in Massachusetts. Its origins can be traced to 1995. The website is www.constantcontact.com. Since 2008, the company has been listed on Deloitte's technology Fast 500 list.

There are 3 plans. For up to 500 contacts, there is a plan that has a free 60-day trial. The Basic Plan Price can range from $20 per month to $295 a month, depending on the number of contacts. The Email Plus plan ranges from $45 to $295. The other plan ranges from $195 to $595.

In each category, the maximum number may increase depending on your volume of subscribers. For example in the Personal Marketer Plan, up to 50 000 subscribers cost $595 per month. If you have more subscribers, you will have to contact them for pricing. Depending on which plan you have, you will have various image storage. They offer webinars, and there are community forums, blogs, and articles to assist you.

Limitations

It is more costly than other ESPs.

Reports are basic and not as advanced and extensive as other ESPs. However if you are starting out this will be satisfactory.

There is an additional fee for preparing and emailing surveys.

Benefits

The company's email support and telephone support are available for longer hours than other ESP on weekdays and they are available on weekends too. Live chat is available on weekdays.

AWeber

This company was established in 1998 and it is ideal for companies with smaller email lists who prefer to send many follow-up emails. The website is www.aweber.com and it is located in Pennsylvania.

There is a 30-day trial for lists with up to 500. Pricing plans range from $19 for up to 500 subscribers to $149 per month for up to 25 000 subscribers. Technical support is available by email, phone, and live chat.

Benefits

The interface is easy to use.

Follow-up autoresponders are available.

They provide segmentation lists

There is unlimited image hosting with access to over 6000 images.

They provide good reporting.

Chat support is available on weekends.

There are informative articles, tutorials, live webinars and guides available.

Limitations

More costly than others if you are on a budget.

Vertical Response

This company was established in 2001 and is located in California. The website is www.verticalresponse.com. They have received many awards throughout the years and was on the Inc. 5000 list of America's fastest growing companies for 8 years.

Email Marketing

There are free plans. If you wish to pay as you go, you can pay according to the number of emails you send. Therefore if you only will send emails occasionally this is a better option for you. For example up to 500 000 emails cost 0.75 cents each. If you have less emails to send, there are various price ranges.

On the other plans, you can pay $11 monthly and up to $250 monthly depending on the number of subscribers. On the Pro Plan, you pay $16 monthly and up to $363 monthly. There are introductory price discounts available.

Benefits

Reporting is good.

Technical support is reliable and options include phone, email, and live chat. You can obtain email and live chat support on weekends.

Video tutorials, articles, information on blogs and live webinars are available.

Limitations

Depending on which platform you use there may be limits. VR2 one of its platforms does not have a media library. However, the Classic Plan gives you 25 MB storage and access to thousands of royalty-free images.

Minimal features. For example, you won't be able to wrap text around an image or use spell check. If you want more advanced features, use another ESP.

No Spam Checker is available.

No advanced segmentation lists is available.

There are limited customization templates.

MailChimp

It is located in Georgia and was established in 2001. The website is www.mailchimp.com. There is a fee plan and two basic paid plans. For the free plan, you are allowed up to 2000 subscribers and can send up to 12,000 emails per month. On the free plan there are no autoresponders, spam filter tools, or email testing. You will also have the MailChimp brand on your email.

The other plans are pay-as-you-go and monthly plans. You can pay from $0.005 - $0.03 per email, depending on the number of subscribers. The company offers additional services such as Social Pro a resource tool that can collect public data about your subscribers such as social sites, age and gender.

Benefits

Unlimited image storage is free with every plan.

It is simple to understand.

There are many themes to choose from.

Strong reporting is provided.

The free plan is very popular.

There is great segmentation on your paid plans and you can deliver emails by time zone.

There are great add-ons and integration.

Limitations

No telephone support is available. Other forms of technical support are available and also inquiries on their Twitter and Facebook page are answered quickly.

If you are transferring lists there is a re-opt-in process in certain situations.

Company Checklist

Besides the factors that are discussed above, when selecting an ESP, also note these matters:

Read the company's Terms and Conditions.

Know what you will get for your package.

Know what the company's refund policy is.

Ensure there are no hidden charges. Some companies' year is tallied at 365 days while for others it is 360 days.

Know what will happen should you decide to cancel.

Check the company's security page.

Email Marketing Best Training Programs

Now that you are more knowledgeable about what is involved, you may consider marketing training. These listed will offer you a practical and enjoyable learning experience.

Online Marketing Institute

The website is www.onlinemarketinginstitute.org. You will learn the essentials of email marketing while learning about the latest trends.

Email Success Summit

Email Success Summit is a course that offers 7 phases of email marketing. Topics include developing your lists, traffic & lead magnets, copywriting, building relationships, campaigns, deliverability and profiting among other topics. You will obtain a free marketing pack and starter guide after which you can pay for the course. The website is www.emailsuccesssummit.com.

Lynda

The website is www.lynda.com. There are many email marketing courses with over 300 video tutorials.

Market Motive

The website is www.marketmotive.com and the course is designed to make you a proficient email marketer. Topics include email as a conversation, metrics, marketing automation, mailing lists and landing pages and working with an ESP.

Hubspot Academy

The website is academy.hubspot.com. After gaining knowledge from your training, you can become certified. There are various levels of certification.

MarketingProfs

The website is www.marketingprofs.com. It is established by a marketing professor and other professors share ideas and resources. They provide practical and hands-on experience.

Founder, CEO and Marketing Professor Allan Weiss, established it in 2000. He is a professor at the University of Southern California. He also taught previously at Stanford University.

Summary

When making your options consider whether the program is tailored to your needs. Some programs cater to small business owners whereas for others they cater for large companies. If you wish to track your success, find out what measurement the various companies use. Some training programs offer certification. You also have to factor in the cost of your program.

Chapter 5

How to Start

Step 1. Sign up for an ESP

You have your website or blog. You are ready to market your product or service. Where do you begin?

Your first step is to select a dependable email service provider (ESP) and sign up for an account. I provided you with several of them in the previous chapter. There are many others, but by now you know what services you need. Be very vigilant and focused when selecting an email service provider. If you select one and then have to change to another, it can be time-consuming and frustrating depending on the procedure that has to be followed in order to make that transition.

Let us examine what services your ESP should offer.

Be able to track and report on open rates and click-through rates

Your open rate is the term given when people on your email list open your email. The rate is usually given as a percentage. For example, if 4 people are on your list and 1 person opens it, then your open rate is 25%. Your click through rate (CTR) is the number of users who clicked on the link in your email.

Click through rates

Your email click-through rate is the number of users who clicked the links in your email and is taken to your blog, website or where ever you wish to direct them. The more clicks you obtain the more effective is your marketing campaign.

Track your unsubscribe information

Your subscribers signed up to receive your notifications and emails. They may also wish to unsubscribe. Ensure that when they have changed their settings, your ESP will make the necessary changes. It can be very irritating for an individual to receive particular emails after they have already unsubscribed.

Regulate your opt-in and opt-out process

Opt-in means that a subscriber has chosen to receive your email. A subscriber can opt-out meaning he no longer wishes to receive your information.

Opting-out and Unsubscribe

Opting-out means that the person does not want any emails from your company or from you. Unsubscribe means that the individual is no longer interested in receiving emails about that particular event or topic.

These are two examples that highlight the differences.

If you no longer wish to receive emails about our herbal remedies, click the link below. (Unsubscribe)

If you no longer wish to receive emails from John Doe, click the link below. (Opt-Out)

Ensure that you allow individuals to select the boxes for themselves. Do not have pre-checked boxes. Many times, individuals do not read the fine print. If you have pre-checked boxes where you express for example that other affiliate companies can email them, or you can send them information about your other brands, they may be surprised when they receive them as they did not sign-up. This is a tactic used by other marketers but in the long run it can affect how your subscribers view you. Therefore be upfront and let them decide for themselves by checking the boxes.

Additionally, do not combine your subscribers. If you have various brands, do not lump all as one and send emails out to everyone as if they all signed up for the same thing. You can recommend and inform them about your other products but allow them to sign-up and indicate what they wish to know more about.

Complies with the CAN-SPAM Act of 2003.

The full name of the act is the Controlling the Assault of Non-Solicited Pornography and Marketing Act and it was passed in the USA in 2003.

Email Service Providers will require you to have an unsubscribe link in your campaigns and that your contact information and address be visible. You will also be required to abide by anti-spam laws of the countries where your subscribers reside. Do not be overwhelmed as the information is all online. All you have to do is type in the country and anti-spam laws and you can obtain information on what is required.

Additionally, some ESPs require you to inform them where you received your email lists. There are operators referred to as lead vendors that offer contact names to companies. You can rent a mailing list or you can purchase a mailing list. With the rental of a list, you are permitted to use contact inventory of a third party but they send the emails on your behalf. When you purchase a mailing list you may have a limit on the time frame in which you can use it but you have access to the actual names. Unlike the rental of a list, when you purchase a list, you can actually see the email addresses.

Offer compatible templates for mobile users

Many individuals check their emails on their phone more often than their desktop. You should ensure that your ESP offers templates that are user-friendly on mobile phones. Have you ever tried to go to a website using your mobile phone and half the screen is obscure? Or sometimes you try to click on a link and seconds later you are still clicking but nothing happens? You do not want this to happen to your recipients. Ensure that the templates offered allows mobile users to have a good experience.

The template that is shown next, is template Wooshi. It has a grid-based layout with eye-catching visuals and text.

The next template is called Underscore which depicts a classic newsletter. There are many sections for news items and parts for more lengthy articles.

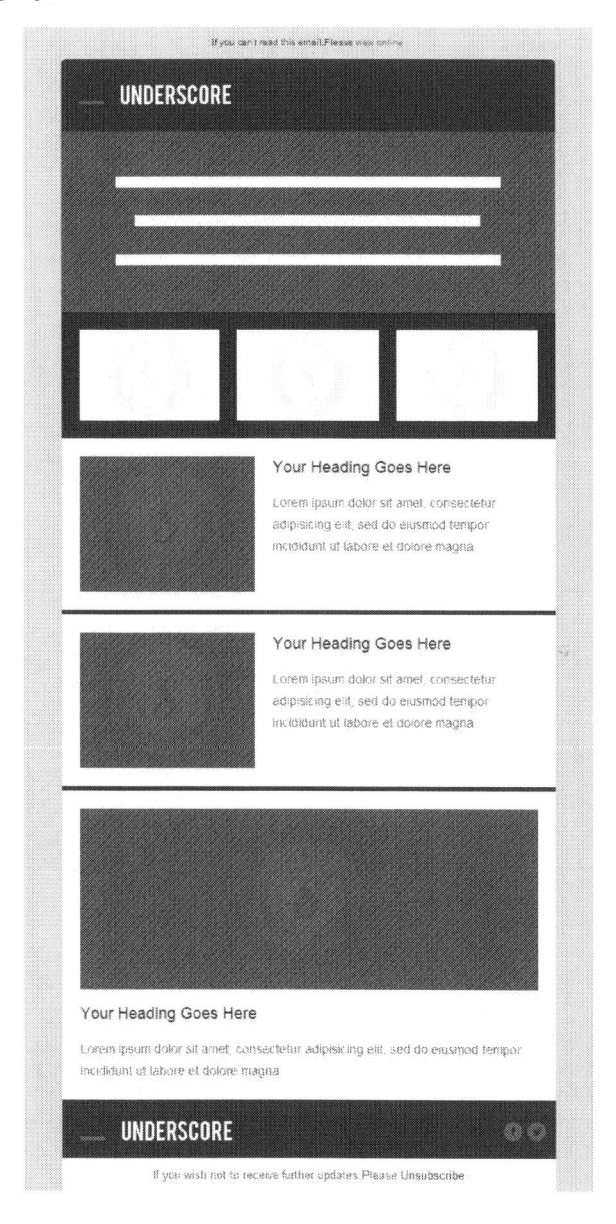

Email Marketing

Template Tubor has a 2 x 2 grid.

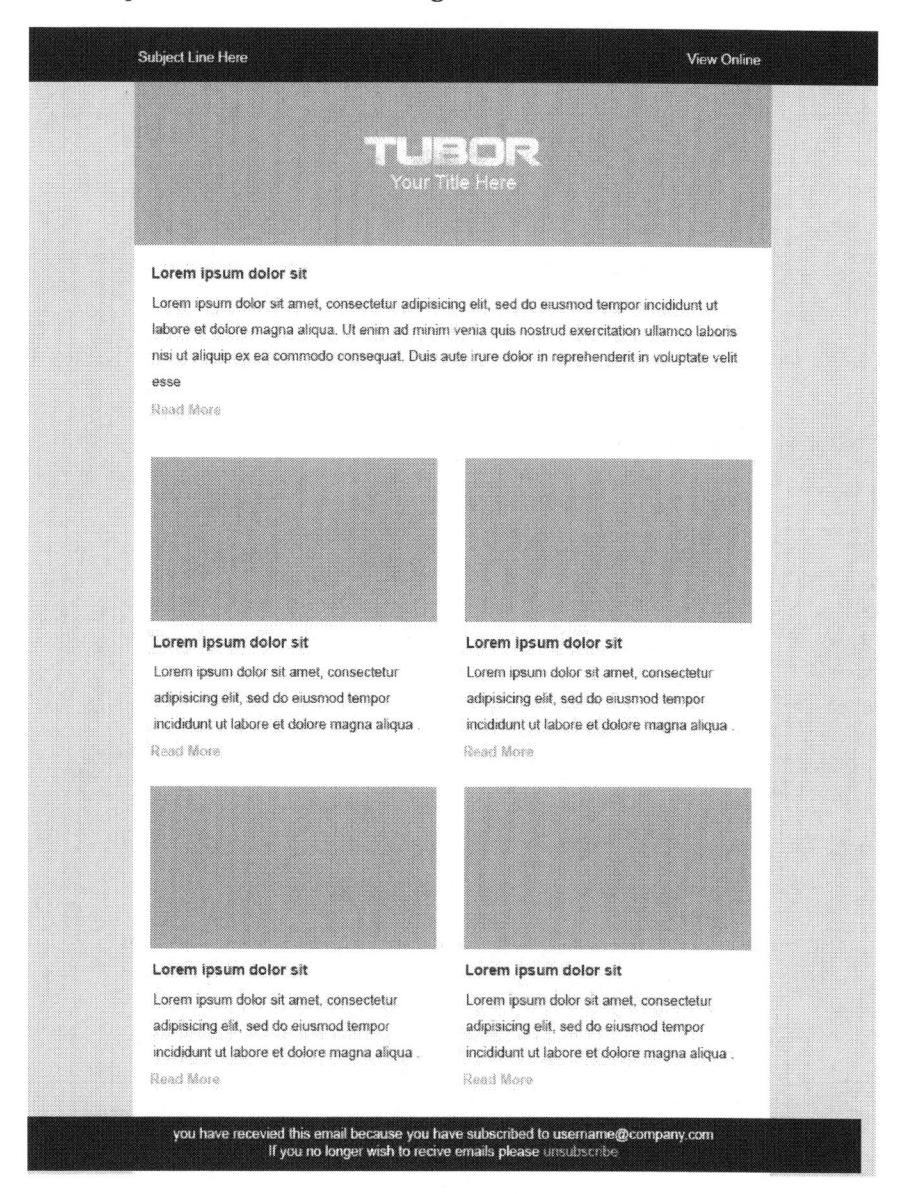

Email Marketing

For your engaging blog updates and newsletter, you can use a colorful template, yet with a sufficient white space design. The next template is known as Tempo.

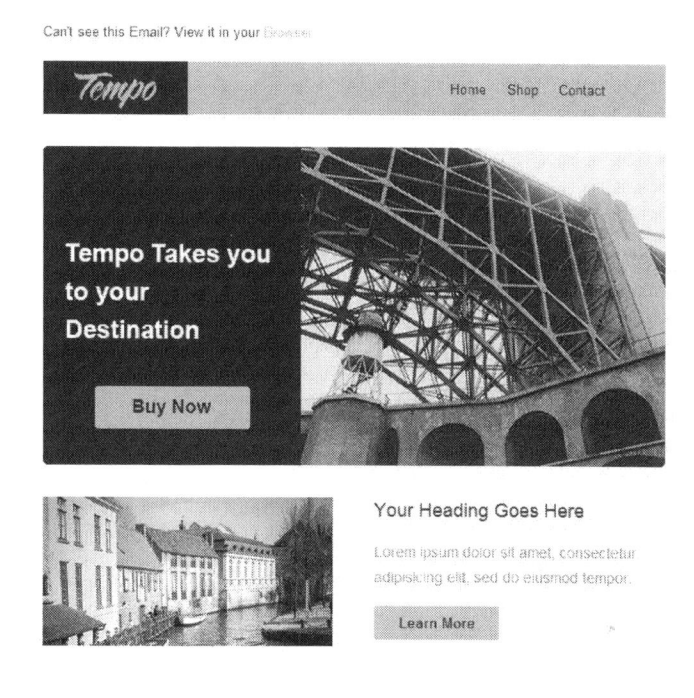

Email Marketing

The Simple design allows your reader's attention to hone in on your product. It is elegant and neat.

52

This template is great for retail businesses.

Reasons for signing up with an ESP

You may wonder why you should sign up with an email service provider when you can simply use email platforms such as Outlook or Google and in the blind copy (bcc) area insert individuals email address.

When you use this option, your messages are more than likely to be tagged as spam and end up in an individual's spam folder instead of his or her inbox. You could be marked as someone who has violated the CAN-SPAM Act. An email service provider, on the other hand, is designed to send bulk emails and eliminate many of your hassles.

An ESP assists you with time management. Subscribers can be added to your lists easily and be removed if they unsubscribe.

Additionally, you will be able to obtain reports on who opened your emails and clicked on them.

Now that you are aware of the importance of having an email service provider, let us further examine what you need to consider when making your selection.

Factors to Consider when Selecting an ESP

Your budget

There are email service providers whose services are free and others that can cost you a couple of hundreds of dollars monthly. It all depends on what you require. Therefore shop around and read the reviews given by other marketers. Examine what is best for you.

Your objectives

If at this stage you have moderate goals, then perhaps you prefer to select an email service provider that offer moderate services. On the other hand, if you have exceptional major goals, you will need an ESP who can cater to your illustrious marketing campaigns. First examine, what your goals are and then let that guide you in making your selection.

Technical support

Base on your goals and the vision you have for your business, determine the level of technical support you will need. If something happens and you have an urgent matter, would you like a 24-hour service or is submitting an email ticket and waiting for a response a day or two later sufficient for you? Examine your options.

The Status of the ESP

Find out all you can about the service provider you wish to do business with. How long has the company been in the business? How is the company rated? Is the company reputable? Choosing your email service provider is not like selecting a new snack on the market. You open the bag and if it is not to your liking you throw it away and get another one. Yes, you can select another but think about the hassle of starting over and the procedures you have to start over with a new company. This is your livelihood so be prudent in your choice.

Delivering Emails

From reading reviews, ensure that the company has a good reputation for delivering emails. It does not make sense for an individual to sign up and then the emails you send end up in your recipient's spam folder or vanish into thin air.

Importing Accessibility

It is always great to plan ahead. If you have signed up with an ESP and later on wish to switch to another, you do not want to have a headache importing your contacts to the new one. To combat this, find out how easy it is to transport your existing list to a new one. For example, depending on whose service you use, you may have to ask your existing subscribers to sign up again. That can cause you to lose some of your existing subscribers who may think the task tedious to sign up again.

User-friendly network

There is nothing more frustrating than signing up for a service and then realizing thereafter, that the tools and resources for you to use, are not as easy to manage as you had thought. You can use the free trial period for those that cost money, to ascertain which interface is easier for you to work with.

Thus, we have examined the main points about Step 1. Sign up for an ESP. You are informed about what you should take into consideration when signing up for an ESP. Let us examine the other steps.

Step 2. Have proper opt-in forms

After you have signed up for an email service provider, ensure you have proper opt-in forms. These are what you will use to invite individuals to join your list. For them to join, you must have a wonderful incentive to offer in exchange for their email addresses. Whatever it is, remember that it must be of value to your subscribers and it should be very enthralling that it cannot be refused.

If you are unsure what to offer, you can offer more than one incentive to increase the likelihood of individuals signing up. This way you will be able to determine what your subscribers prefer. Do not delay in setting yours up.

Single opt-in and Double opt-in

When you inquire if someone wants to receive your emails and they do and sign up to you platform, that is a single opt-in.

A double-opt-in differs as after they sign up, a confirmation email is sent and inside that email is a link. Once the person clicks the link agreeing that it is okay for you to send more emails, the information is saved on your provider's system. The double opt-in is more popular as it gives extra proof of consent. Ensure that your ESP has this functionality if you would like to have this service.

Step 3. Develop your Email List

Your next step is to build your email list. These are various ways to do so. Here we list some examples:

Host an entertaining webinar where you can collect emails addresses at registration.

Market using social media. For example, make use of your Facebook page to publicize what you have to offer. Include a call-to-action button to your Facebook business page. Use Twitter, LinkedIn, Pinterest, YouTube, Google + Page and other social media platforms. Add social sharing buttons to your website pages. Promote an online competition which requires signing up.

Promote your stuff as a guest on someone's blog.

Step 4. Keep in touch by offering great content

As your list grows, ensure that you send engaging content to your subscribers regularly. Pay attention to the pitfalls that we have already discussed. You can also set up what is known as an autoresponder.

Autoresponders are emails that you write in advance and set up to email at intervals. Rather than emailing at the specific time and sending out, you can plan them ahead. While you are relaxing or working on other projects, the emails will be sent to your subscribers at your pre-set time.

Your autoresponder can be a welcome message that is sent to your subscriber upon signing up. It can be a five part series on recipes that feature pumpkin as the ingredient. It can even be a series on how to live a more positive life.

Reasons for using autoresponders

It allows you to promote you valuable content, even those you have in your archives.

It ensures that your new subscribers have the same delightful experience as those who are not so new.

You can mention great offers.

It's a way to allow your subscribers to trust you.

It allows your subscribers to be more familiar with your brand.

You may wonder what topics you can share with your lists. Here are some things that you can explore.

Ideas

Offer advice on topics you are knowledgeable about. You can give tips which they can use to make their life so much easier. For example you can share great ideas on how to organize their home so that they have more space available. Or how to break a bad habit.

Reveal inspiring stories about yourself. Give them more insight about what led you to start your business.

Ask questions that will provoke a response. Invite your subscribers to share memorable stories and express their opinions on a particular topic or event.

Address challenges that many people face.

Present them with informative resources and tools to make their lives easier.

Now that you have various ideas, you can plan ahead. Figure out how many messages you would like to have and at what interval you would like to send them.

Tips

Do not mislead or fool anyone

If you communicated with your subscribers that you will give away something for free, do so. You would have already increase their level of expectation and if you do not deliver, the trust they had for you will diminish.

Moreover, ensure that the link you provide for them to download the free document or report is not faulty. Also ensure that the document or resource is in a format which they can easily use and open.

Be engaging

Do not be dull in your communication. Allow your warmth to be felt by your subscribers. Complement your brand. For example, if your website is geared towards humor and in your autoresponders, your tone is boring, it will be a stark contrast to what your subscribers expect of you.

Share knowledge

You do not have to be an encyclopedia or act like an austere librarian. You can be warm and engaging but share the things you learned.

Have an ongoing conversation

You can allow your subscribers answer and share their opinions on your website. Inform them about the other social media platforms that you are on, should they wish to communicate with you on those platforms too.

Things to Avoid

Do not send a welcome correspondence and nothing else. It's like someone visiting your home, and you warmly welcome her with open arms and then leave her standing by the door while you sit on the couch engrossed in the television. From the warm welcome, your visitor would have expected that you would have maintain your focus on her visitation. It's the same way when you send a welcome message. Your subscribers are waiting to hear more from you.

Do not send many autoresponders daily. The objective is to send them at normal intervals. Your intervals should not be spaced 4 hours apart. It's like someone ringing your phone to convey a message which she have appreciated. Then half an hour later, the same person calls again. Then twenty minutes later a call comes in again. You will lessen your effectiveness if you dilute your messages or annoy your subscribers.

Remember that it is a business you have. Do not confuse your business with your friends, family, doctor, therapist or counsellor. The things you should only say to those in your inner circle, do not share with your subscribers. Have you ever been in a public setting and a stranger starts talking about certain issues that should remain private? Or, it can even be someone you know, like a coworker who rants about personal matters on the job. I'm sure you have instances where it makes you feel uncomfortable when individuals talk about certain details, which you do not want to hear. Similarly, do not make your subscribers uncomfortable by divulging information that is not relevant or will startle your audience.

Do not set up your autoresponder so that it coincides with your other notifications. For example, if you send your newsletters out every Tuesday, send your autoresponder on another day of the week.

Do not oversell your product and service. Do not turn every message into a plea for your subscribers to purchase what you have to offer.

Step 5. Provide frequent offers

Not only should you send great content, but once you have developed a good relationship, you should also provide offers on a frequent basis.

Email marketing is not a process that once you put certain systems in place, then the work is over. It requires constant monitoring and adaptation. You cannot be stagnant. Evolve and frequently assess what is best for your business and customers.

What to have on your website or blog

Ensure that your subscribers know, that you do not plan to use their information for any other purposes. Place a declaration that communicates to your subscribers and customers that their information is safe. You can place this declaration next to where subscribers will place their email address, so it can be seen quite prominently.

To promote your brand, insert a banner or logo at the top of your website and communication. When using it in your newsletter, ensure that it is not blurry and it is the correct size.

If you do not have a logo at this point, there are online sources where you can use images. Observe the rules pertaining to intellectual property. Many sources allow you to use images for free.

Ask your friends for feedback and opinions about your website or blog. This way you can eliminate any errors that may be on your site.

Your color scheme should be soothing and engaging. Be consistent with how you use colors and fonts. Make sure that individuals can see your links. If your background color is dark and your link is in a dark color, individuals may not be able to view it. You want your readers to enjoy their time viewing your website and reading your information instead of squinting and zooming in and out to figure out what the words are.

Chapter 6

What to Include in Your Emails

Include a proper "from" and "reply-to address"

Yes, you are sending an email but this is not an email to the people who already know you. Therefore, your tone and your words must be selected carefully. There are some other details which you must pay attention to.

Choose your "from" information and "reply to" address. You subscriber will want to know who the email is from and depending on what address is given, a subscriber will decide what action to take. It is best to place an individual's name. You can include your business name too but it should have the name and the company's name.

Whatever address you use, ensure that the email address you choose is valid and you frequently examine your emails.

Have an engaging subject line

Your subject line is what determine if your subscribers will click on your email and read it in its entirety. You need to arouse their curiosity. Additionally, you can have a customized template where you can include your subscriber's name. You will have to examine and maintain your list nonetheless as it is still your responsibility to do so. This is to avoid an email being sent to a subscriber stating, "Hello (Name Error)." Instead, you will want it to say "Hello Mary".

The wording of your email should inspire subscribers to open the email right away. Also, do not mislead your subscribers. Otherwise, they will only mistrust you. One way in which you can mislead them is if you have a topic as your subject, but when the email is opened, there is nothing in the content that explains or discusses the topic you mentioned.

Introduction

It is your choice if you wish to include a greeting. It is not compulsory. However, an introduction is a way to allow your personality to shine through in the early stages.

Unsubscribe link

Make sure you have an option for your subscribers to unsubscribe. Place it in an area where your subscribers can see it.

Have plain text

Very often, you will see the acronym HTML which means Hypertext Markup Language. Web pages and email templates are programmed in such a way that you can format your text and images. On the other hand, plain text is normal text with no formatting choices. HTML enhances the appearances as you can use graphics, colors, links and columns.

HTML is great to use if you would like to present your information in such a way that you wish to entice your subscribers to purchase your offer. However, if the code is not done properly, your email can be identified as spam. As mentioned before, if subscribers change their settings so they do not receive images, your HTML email will not be visible to your readers.

Thus the viable option is to send both an HTML email and a plain text version. Some email providers make it compulsory for you to include a plain text version also before you can send emails.

Be mobile-friendly

Have a design that is pleasant for your mobile users. Ensure your images have the correct size. Have your call to action link formatted so that mobile users can easily tap on it from their mobile phone. Have space between links so your email is not congested. You want to make sure that your mobile users can click each link easily without having to tap repeatedly and zooming in and out in frustration.

The Content

Use short paragraphs so that your subscriber can easily scan the content of your email. If you are using images, make sure that they are not large. Be mindful of your mobile users, as large images will take a while to download. You may have to scale your images so that they are the appropriate sizes.

For subscribers who has set their email setting to block images, ensure that you have the alternative text. This is a way that subscribers can read what you wish to convey. Avoid using unsuitable names for your images in the ALT text.

You can choose to send a traditional newsletter on a regular basis such as weekly or monthly. You can include links to your website or information you gathered from other websites, along with photographs, coupons or special offers. Whatever your schedule, you must ensure that you maintain it regularly. Do not send one weekly and then three months later you send the next one. By then interest in what you have to say will wan and people may unsubscribe.

Refrain from using background images as not every individual may have the settings on his or her device to view them. You can use background color though but ensure that it complements your brand and design.

Note, however, that formatting a newsletter can take up much of your time so you may decide to pay someone to design it for you. If you know that your schedule does not allow for newsletters or you are a habitual procrastinator, be very selective with how often you send them out or you may decide not to use this route altogether.

Instead of sending newsletters, an alternative is to send digest emails. It is an email with notifications you wish to inform your subscribers about. It is a shortened version of a newsletter. With newsletters, though your subscribers may find it intriguing, they may not have the time to read all the contents right away so they may put it in a folder where they can read it later. Then they may forget to return to read it as their inboxes are filled with other emails that they wish to read. With digest emails, your subscribers can quickly scan the contents and click on the links.

Digest emails are easier to create than newsletters and hone your subscribers' attention on your content.

With notifications, however, if you do not have content to post frequently, then you won't email much. When your subscribers do not hear from you, they will unsubscribe. If you only wish to use one option, you will have to get to know your audience better and decide whether a newsletter or notification is better to promote your business and keep your readers satisfied.

The good news is that you can use both if you are not sure what to do. That way you can examine what your subscribers prefer after assessing your reports.

Have a call to action

In your content, individuals should be aware of what you would like them to do after reading your emails. Whether you want them to download something or signup for something for example. Always ensure that you effectively communicate what you want them to do.

Footer

If you are in the USA, the CAN-SPAM Act stipulates what information should be given in the footer. Your address must be included in the footer, whether it is a post office box, private box or current physical address. Ensure that your address is current and doesn't reflect where you use to live years ago.

Utilize the spam checker

Some email providers offer a spam checker. The spam checker checks for words that may prompt spam filters. By using the spam checker, it increases the likelihood of your email being delivered to the inbox of your recipients. There are free spam checkers available online if the service provider you select doesn't have one.

Send an email test

As you check your email, read carefully and look for mistakes. Are the "from" field and the "reply to" field information correct? Are the images the right size and convey what you wish to communicate? Do your links work? Is the preview text persuasive so that your readers will click to read more?

Before leaving home, you usually check yourself in the mirror to ensure your appearance is presentable to the public. One sure way to test the appearance of your emails is to send yourself the email to view how it will look to your subscribers. Your email service provider should have the feature of sending yourself a test version.

Chapter 7

Marketing Concepts

Drip Marketing

Drip marketing terminology is based on the agricultural process known as drip irrigation. In agriculture, it includes using small amounts of water to sustain plants over a prolonged period in order to produce a regular crop. It saves fertilizer and water and is operated through narrow tubes to deliver water directly to the roots of different plants.

Likewise, drip marketing or drip campaign involves sending efficient pre-set messages to your subscribers to nurture your prospects.

Types of Drip Campaigns

Top-Of-Mind Drips

As the name suggests, it keeps your business at the forefront of your subscribers' minds by keeping them engaged.

Educational Drips

This type of drip is information you provide to your subscribers to prepare them to purchase your product or service.

Re-engagement Drips

These are emails you employ to win back your subscribers whose interest has diminished.

Competitive Drips

These target your competitors' customers. You entice them by highlighting the advantages of using your product or service.

Promotional Drips

You entice potential customers with promotions and special offers.

Training Drips

Training resources is provided to new subscribers or to advance your subscribers from one level to the next level of a training program.

50/50 Split Test

Sometimes you will see the term 50/50 split test. It means that you subject half of your subscribers to a version of an email or landing page and the next half to a different version or landing page and comparing to see which version does betters. This is to help guide you in future objectives.

10/10/80 Split Test

The 10/10/80 split test is the same thing just that you expose 10% to one thing, the other 10% and 80% to a different version.

A/B Testing

A/B testing is another term used to mean the same thing. You divide your subscribers into two groups A and B and observe which group performs better after sending different resources.

ALT Text

ALT text means alternative text. When an image is blocked and the subscriber hovers over the image, text is still displayed. In this way, the recipient will still be able to know what to do or what the image is about, though the image is blocked.

Rich Email Content

Rich email content is using advanced technology such as are videos, podcasts and other email matter that subscribers can view without leaving their inbox.

Role-based Email Address

Role-based email address is an address that starts with sales@, info@, press@ or any other description which reveals that messages you send to the address may be seen by or forwarded to more than one individual.

Share With Your Network

Share With Your Network (SWYN) means that subscribers can add content from your email to their social media platform so that family, associates and friends in their network can view it.

Onboarding

Onboarding is the procedure where you acquaint new subscribers with your brand and email platform by utilizing your signup confirmation page and welcome correspondence.

Subscriber Lifecycle

Subscriber lifecycle is the different stages a subscriber undergoes. It depicts the timeline from the moment the subscriber signed up until the moment they unsubscribe or cease to receive your emails. Included are the stages of acquisition, onboarding, engagement, super-engagement, reengagement, and transition.

Swipe File

Swipe file is a file of your highly performing emails, calls to action, landing pages, subject lines and other elements that you refer to for inspiration and knowledge.

Targeting

Targeting means emailing the right correspondence to the right individual at the right time.

Throttling

Throttling is when an internet service provider decelerates the rate at which an email is delivered to subscribers.

Co-Registration

Co-Registration is the procedure of using partners to obtain opt-in leads so you can include in your mailing list. How it works is that your partners will inquire from new registrants if they wish to receive information from your brand or company. If they opt-in they will be added to your list. Thereafter you can market directly to them.

List Scrubbing/Pruning/List Cleaning

This terminology refers to keeping your email list tidy and devoid of defunct email addresses or typos. If you do not do this regularly, the bad email addresses can cause you to be flagged as sending potential spam. Moreover your data reporting will be affected. For example you may think that you have the emails of 500 subscribers. However, if half of the email addresses are defunct or have an improper spelling, your total sent emails will be less than initially assumed.

Permission Marketing

Permission Marketing is the process where goods and services are marketed to prospective customers who have consented to receiving your marketing information. One example is opt-in emails.

Conclusion

Thank you again for purchasing this book!

I hope this book was able to help you to have a broader understanding of the email marketing process. Many companies and organizations use various marketing methods to meet their goals. Explore and test all your options to ascertain which ones work best for you. Be flexible with your marketing methods. Do not limit yourself. Technology is an evolving process with more software and applications becoming more available.

Pay special attention to your audience. Your subscribers have various needs and interests. Therefore analyze your data and effectively create various strategies you will implement to influence them to purchase what you have to offer. Provide invigorating, relevant and dynamic content. Your audience should be delighted to receive your correspondence. Remember that it is an ongoing process so do not be frustrated when you do not see immediate results. Your subscribers are knowledgeable and you will have to offer valuable information and make the connection before they are influenced to make a purchase. Therefore, build your brand and develop a bond with your subscribers.

Make the commitment to implement great business practices. The more you deliver on your promises the more your subscribers will trust you. Request your readers' involvement. Include social media buttons on your website and in your emails so the dialogue can continue on other platforms. Genuinely care about your audience.

This is the best email marketing era because information is readily available and you have many avenues to obtain new subscribers and promote your business. You are well equipped and quite capable of surpassing your highest expectations! Once you apply what I have shared with you, you will be a successful contender and a notable email marketer.

Email Marketing:

Strategies to Capture and Engage Your Audience, While Quickly Building an Authority

Table of Contents

Introduction 81

Chapter 1: Everything You Should Know About
               Email Marketing 83

Chapter 2: The Importance of Being an Authority 93

Chapter 3: Getting Started Building Your Authority 95

Chapter 4: Intermediate Authority Building 109

Chapter 5: Advanced Authority Building 119

Chapter 6: Tips for Improving Your Metrics 127

Chapter 7: Popular Email Marketing Platforms 131

Conclusion 135

Introduction

Congratulations on purchasing *Email Marketing: Strategies to Capture and Engage Your Audience, While Quickly Building an Authority* and thank you for doing so. Email marketing has received a bad reputation over the years on both sides of the equation. Marketers have turned away from it as a fad that is past its prime and many would-be subscribers are wary of it because of the potential for fraud.

This is not necessarily the case, however and the following chapters will discuss ways in which you can ensure that subscribers are always looking forward to your emails by ensuring that they view you as an authority on the matter. The benefits of being an authority in relation to a given niche, are much the same as any other authority figure, when you speak everyone will listen, and if you follow the outline suggested in the following chapters you will go from uneducated layman to first and foremost authority in your field. Your journey begins now.

There are plenty of books on this subject on the market, thanks again for choosing this one! Every effort was made to ensure it is full of as much useful information as possible, please enjoy!

Chapter 1

Everything You Should Know About Email Marketing

While it may appear as though public opinion has turned when it comes to the general success rate of email marketing, the reality of the matter is that when done properly, email marketing is still one of the most powerful marketing tools in an online marketer's toolbox. The guiding reason behind this fact is the same that it has always been, it is successful because it appears more personal when it comes to a customer's private space (their inbox). As long as the email is sent with permission, studies show that email is the marketing channel that is most preferred by consumers nearly 2 to 1 over both mobile and social media marketing.

This means it is also still the most cost-effective way to reach potential customers bar none, with the Direct Marketing Association estimating that its return on investment is a staggering 4,000 percent. Email marketing is so effective for the cheap and easy way it allows you to reach consumers on the regular but it will only be so if you take the time to become an authority in your niche and provide useful content in your emails, outside of just a list of the latest deals. From there, the quality of the content will become more well-known and the number of subscribers will grow, ultimately leading to more sales as a result.

This doesn't mean that any type of email newsletter will ultimately lead to results as it is easy for any email from a business or website to be marked as spam regardless of how much useful information it may contain. This is why it is important to moderate your pitches and only include them as a part of a value exchange between yourself and your subscribers. The implied agreement is this, you promise not to send out a constant stream of newsletters and only include things that show you value your subscriber's limited time; and in return, your subscribers agree to continue receiving and looking at the emails you send, and the appropriate amount of advertising and no more.

Building this trust is a difficult row to hoe as you will inherently start out at a disadvantage because your potential subscribers have all been burned before, guaranteed. This doesn't mean it is impossible, however, it just means that your emails need to include effective subject lines and have a distinctive voice while always provide information that the niche you target is sure to care about.

Build an email marketing strategy

Creating an effective email newsletter week after week and year after year can only happen if you take the time to create the right email marketing strategy for your company before you ever send out your first email. To do so you will need to understand what email marketing means for you and your business as it can easily mean different things for different people. You will also need to set realistic goals when it comes to determining what your end goal is, form a list based on your end goal, determine how content will be generated and figure out just what it is all going to cost.

Decide what email marketing means for you

For the purposes of this book, email marketing can be thought of as permission-based communication between you and your users or customers with the overall goal of increasing customer retention and ultimately improving sales. The most important thing to remember as you begin your email marketing journey is that without getting permission, all you are creating is more spam that will be deleted without ever being opened. This means you will need to be very vigilant when it comes to building your list of willing subscribers and never take the easy way out and buy an email list from a bulk provider of such things.

Beyond this definition, it is also important to begin your email marketing journey by clearing determining just what email marketing is going to mean for your website or business in particular. Doing so will allow you to proceed in such a way that maximizes the impact of your emails to ensure the most market penetration possible. If you aren't quite sure what your end goal should ultimately be, it may help to choose your goals as describe below first and then revisit your larger plans.

Pick your goals

When it comes to determining your goals in regards to your future email marketing campaign, you will want to ask yourself several questions.

- How will marketing via email relate to your broader marketing goals?
- Will the various marketing efforts intertwine or simply be related?
- How are you currently attracting visitors?
- How do you want email marketing to generate new customers or visitors?
- How frequently do you want to connect with your subscribers?

Once you have answered these questions you will want to ensure the goals you picked are SMART as well as relevant.

- *Your goals should be specific:* If your goals related to your email marketing campaign are specific, you will be able to clearly explain them in only a few sentences. You should have a clear idea of the various requirements for achieving the goal as well as what types of constraints, if any, may stand between you and the completion of the goal. You should also feel as though the goal has a clear timeline as well as if you will need any outside help to complete it.

- *Your goals should be measurable:* If a goal is measureable, you will be able to clearly determine if your campaign has been either a resounding success, acceptable or a huge mistake. You should also be able to split the goal up into smaller pieces which can all then also be measured for success or failure to keep you firmly on the path to success.

- *Your goals should be attainable:* Attainable goals are those that accurately take into account anything standing between you and the successful completion of the goal in question (such as the inherent bias against email marketing). It is important to take a look at your goal from all sides and be realistic when it comes to determining what might stand in your way. Looking at your goal with rose colored glasses won't help, it is in your best interest to be as critical as possible.

- *Your goals should be realistic:* A goal is realistic if it is attainable, regardless of the amount of effort required, without requiring an act of divine intervention to see them through. The ideal goal is one that is difficult enough that you will have to work for it, but not so difficult that it becomes unrealistic. Likewise, it is important to not pick easy goals as studies show that believing a goal is easily within reach is actually a detriment to your motivation to complete it.

- *Your goal should have a timetable that is clearly defined:* Even the best goals are likely to fall apart if they have a time table that is either too strict or too generous. If a timeline is unreasonably short than you run the risk of having to cut corners to see it through to completion, while on the other hand, timelines that are too lenient don't provide the proper motivation to give them your full attention in the present. As such, finding the appropriate middle ground is the only realistic path to success.

Analyze current process

When it comes to setting goals, you may find it helpful to take a closer look at how you are generating new viewers to your site or customers to your store. In broad strokes, you are likely as concerned with non-customers as you are your actual customers as they are the ones who need to be turned. When done properly, this is exactly the sort of thing that your future email newsletter will be able to help strengthen, but only if you are aware of where the current weak links in the interaction chain currently are.

If you are currently operating an online store that only leads to a confirmation page after a sale has been made and nothing else, then you are essentially shortchanging all the time and effort you likely spend marketing your site. Additionally, this type of transaction tends to feel impersonal from a customer's perspective which makes them less likely to consider coming back in the future. What's more, you lose out again on those who might come to the site but need a little more time before they pull the trigger.

On the other hand, including email marketing into the equation allows you to both potentially track existing customers while at the same time getting information about prospective customers to help keep your store on their minds when the time comes for them to actually buy something. While you certainly won't get everyone to give up additional personal information easily, you are still taking the first step when it comes to building the type of relationship that can turn first time customer into lifetime customers. Additionally, it will provide you additional feedback as you can see how your core audience responds to the individual information in each email and drive new traffic to your site at the same time when those emails are passed along.

Generate the right list

Once you have a clear idea of where you are and where you want to be, you will want to put some serious time and commitment into cultivating the right list of emails to start producing content for on a regular basis. If you have been running a website or store for any length of time you likely have some of the information required for many of your most loyal customers or users. Once you know what you have, you will want to determine how best to acquire the rest of the information you need.

While creating a space on your site that allows interested parties to sign up for your newsletter is a great place to start, you should also include the option during the purchase process as well as suggest it if a user or customer looks at multiple pages of your site in a row. If you already have a core user base before setting up an email newsletter, then this is the one and only time it is acceptable to send out an unsolicited email, simply explaining that you are starting a newsletter and wanted to let your most valued users/customers know. You can only do this once, however, so don't waste the opportunity.

When it comes to gathering data on customers and users, you will want to try and get them to provide you with their general demographics information including things like age, income, location, number of children and marital status. Additionally, you will want to determine their specific interests as they relate to your site as well as their purchase history and anything else you might need to know that is unique to your niche. In many cases, you will be able to break down your list into subgroups, which allows for even more targeting information.

Consider how you will collect data

Once you have a clear idea of what type of information you want from your users or customers, the next thing you will need to determine is how to go about getting it. Sometimes it may be the right choice to ask for it all at once while other times you will want to spread out the process and ask for it in less intrusive chunks. Depending on your needs and those of your audience, there are many different ways you can go about collecting important information including:

- On the confirmation page for successful subscriptions.
- In the email that goes out to new subscribers once they have subscribed.
- Every few months as a newsletter questionnaire.
- With subscriber information update reminders sent out a few times per year.

Additionally, you will want to include certain ties to your newsletter in other ways as well. Most importantly, you will want to include an expressly stated option for subscribers to send the newsletter to their friends. It is important that the option be obvious and expressly stated, even though forwarding an email is always an options because being directly confronted with the option makes it more likely that your subscribers will utilize it. You should also include the link to the signup page in all of your business emails and other advertising material.

With the proper understanding on the type of data that you are going to be collecting, it is important to have a clear idea what you are going to do with it after you have it. All of that data won't do you any good if you don't organize it properly and take advantage of it at every opportunity. Creating the right infrastructure early on is important to ensure certain information doesn't get lost in the shuffle.

Plan for content

While the bulk of the following chapters will help you gain a clearer idea of what to write, when you are first getting started is the perfect time to determine just what type your content creation schedule is going to look like. Especially because you will need to be creating added value for each post, it is important to have a firm idea of what you are going to talk about for at least the first two months so you can see how long it takes you to create the type of content you are looking for. It is likewise important to determine how many pieces of content you will be creating for each newsletter and what products relate to each.

While creating reams of content for your subscribers will be appreciated by some, you should always avoid walls of text for multiple pages. A single, relatively dense page of content is probably enough per newsletter, with that likely being spread out over a few pages, once formatting has been applied. Don't spend all your time working on your newsletter, it is supposed to bring in new business, not consume your business.

Look at the metrics

Once your email newsletter is fully up and running you will want to take a closer look at a number of important metrics to ensure your message is reaching as many people at a time as possible. First and foremost, you will want to be aware of the open rate of your emails, and if you provide the right mix of content and sales then it should be rather high. From there you will want to focus on the number of people who visited your site directly after reading your email which is consider your rate of click throughs. You can also determine how many people did what your email told them to, the source conversions, as well as how many people shared your email with others. Additional information on these metrics and how to improve them can be found in chapter 6.

Chapter 2

The Importance of Being an Authority

As previously discussed, it is extremely important to include plenty of valuable content in each of your newsletters to ensure that subscribers are more likely to open them and stick with them until they get to the part where you are allowed to try and sell them things. The best way to do this is by establishing ethos, nurturing pathos and sealing the deal with logos.

Logos: Logos can be thought of as the reasoning behind the conclusions that you draw as a way of making it seem obvious that they should listen to whatever it is you are saying about the items you are selling. The goal with the marketing portion of your newsletter should be to create hypothetical situations that allow your subscribers to deduce the answer you want them to reach based on the information you provide. The trust that you establish by being an authority is particularly important for logos as it lends additional credibility to the things you say.

Pathos: Pathos can be thought of as the result of logos, and is your goal with email marketing as it can be seen as the swaying of emotions that comes with a powerful argument. Changing a subscriber's pathos is easier once you have built up a relationship that, again, is primarily built on the trust that is gained from you being seen as an expert or authority on the topic in question.

Ethos: Ethos can broadly be thought of as selling yourself or establishing your credibility in the niche in question. Depending on what your niche is, this may or may not be something that you already have. Even if you already have the knowledge, you won't be considered an authority until you share that knowledge to the point that the public perception of the topic considers you a common source. This is something that will only build with time and cannot be rushed, remember slow and steady wins the race.

Authority defined

As such, it is easy to see why building your authority on the niche your business or website caters to is so important when it comes to building your brand both in the short and the long term. Unfortunately, it is easier said than done, especially as there is no surefire way to prove yourself as an authority figure other than to elucidate others on the fact of the matter for long enough to gain the title. Doing so is a mix of generating the right types of leads, having a powerful social media image and being readily visible on Google.

In many situations, the word expert and the word authority are often used interchangeably; this is not the case with online marketing however, as being an authority is everything and being an expert is much worse than simply getting second place. In this case an expert is someone who knows a lot about a certain niche while an authority is the person that all of the experts agree is the first stop for information on a given niche. To put it another way, authorities aren't authorities because they say they are, they are authorities because when they make declarations in regards to their niche of choice, other people listen.

Benefits of authority

The benefits of being an authority in relation to a given niche, are much the same as any other authority figure, when you speak everyone will listen. This is because those who know you are an authority will expect that you know what you are talking about in any given situation, after all, you must know best. It doesn't take much of an imagination to see how this can directly translate into additional sales when given the proper push. If you can reach the status of authority for your niche they you will be able to set the tone for the entire niche as well as have a legion of loyal followers willing to defend everything you say.

When it comes to marketing for your online business or website, it is important to have a healthy social media presence as well as a firm grasp of the importance of SEO if you want to reach out and find new revenue streams. If you also spend time slowly building a reputation as an authority in a given niche, then you will be able to rest easy the revenue streams will come to you instead.

If it seems as though this explanation is giving niche authorities too much credit, take a moment and think of an authority in a given niche that you consider yourself a part of. Odds are you listen when that person renders judgment on something, and you likely follow along without doing the research required to form your own opinion. This is not because you, or anyone who will ultimately listen to you as an authority figure, are less intelligent or more prone to being a follower than anyone else and, in fact, likely shows that you are familiar enough with the niche in question to determine who the authority in question actually is. The point is, once someone has pinpointed an authority figure, they are less likely to apply as much personal judgement to related topics moving forward.

Trust is key

The key in this instance is trust, an authority figure becomes such by being trustworthy, not just a few times, but for long enough that those who follow the authority are comfortable taking anything they say as fact. Taking the time to earn this trust among those who subscribe to your mailing list is crucial to the long term success of your marketing plan as without it you will not the positive metrics, and return on your investment that you are most likely looking for. Once you are able to cultivate this trust it is important to hold it sacrosanct above all else.

Remember, it will take you quite some time to build up the trust of those who read your newsletter, possibly quite some time depending on how crowded the niche you are looking to establish yourself is at the time. However, once you have that trust, something as simple as selling a cheap but ultimately shoddy product and then recommending that your followers purchase it. Even if you weren't aware of the truth of the situation at the time when you made the recommendation, something as simple as this can permanently tarnish your reputation with some followers to the point that you will lose them forever. As such, it is important to value the trust of your subscribers extremely highly and understand exactly what is at stake if you chose to put it at risk in search of profits.

In fact, studies show that the level of trust that a subscriber feels towards the newsletter they are reading, is in direct correlation to how much they feel they can trust the person who is writing the email. As such, before you start building your authority, it is important to ask yourself a few questions to determine if you are presenting yourself in the most trustworthy ways possible. The first thing you need to ask is if you are always doing everything you can to exceed the expectations of your subscribers or customers. A large part of these expectations are likely going to come from your level of accessibility which means that the easier it is for those you are courting to reach you, the better.

Studies show that those who receive personalized emails are 40 percent more likely to at least open the email in question, though this does not necessarily mean just a form "Dear, subscriber name here". In the modern world, most communication tends to be much more impersonal than many people like. As such, taking the time to make little concessions when it comes to personal touches can lead to a significant return on the investment required to make such things a reality.

Part of this personalization should be the personalized attention that you provide to the data of every person who trusts you enough to provide it. While reading through all of this information will provide you valuable data on your most loyal customers, it is equally important to treat that data with the upmost respect when it comes to storing it and never sharing it with any third party sites for any reason. A breach of trust in regards to how data is handled is the cardinal sin of the twenty first century and one that no online business can ever truly recover from. A person who buys things from you regularly who is not treated personally might be a repeat customer, but a repeat customer who is treated in as personalized of a fashion as possible is on their way to becoming a follower.

Chapter 3

Getting Started Building Your Authority

When it comes to using your email newsletter as a platform to build your authority, there are a few things you need to be aware of, the first is how long it is likely going to take to reach your goal and the second is that there are nearly 200 billion emails sent every day, which means that if you want to receive any traction for your marketing attempts you are going to have to stand out from the crowd.

Proper newsletter formatting

When it comes to generating useful content, it is not enough to simply slap it in an email, hit send to all, and be done with it. In fact, there are numerous things to consider before you even get to the actual content generation part of the process.

Personalization: While it would seem as though simply including the name of each subscriber at the start of each newsletter would be enough to make the newsletter feel personalized, in reality this is no longer the case. The high number of spam related emails which include a name, possibly even a first and last name, is enough to make the average person think twice about getting an email that uses their name directly if they do not explicitly know the person involved. This can be a difficult line to navigate as a vague greeting does little to install confidence and a personalized greeting harms trust instead of helping to generate it.

The first place to start is by understanding that the level of familiarity you use when addressing your subscribers should start off around the level reserved for those you know, but only in a formal setting, something like "inaugural subscriber" strikes the right tone for the initial email that you are looking to cultivate. From there it is appropriate for it to grow to something more familiar and less formal over time, but this level of intimacy should be earned and never taken.

While naming conventions can be difficult to pin down, grouping people together based on something individual to that subscriber, such as demographics or even purchase history can immediately put subscribers in a more receptive frame of mind. In fact, studies show that upwards of 90 percent of all customers are likely to open an email that is based around their personalized product history. While this shows that personalization is clearly important, it even more directly emphasis the importance of personalizing in the right way. Remember, it only takes one poorly personalized email to get your email messages marked as spam indefinitely.

Use the right subject lines: As with the greeting of the email, the subject line is the only thing you can actually guarantee every subscriber will see (assuming you make it past their spam filter). According to the experts, the content of your subject line doesn't seem to be as important as the actual length of the subject line itself with the success rates of shorter subject lines rising to the point that those with less than 10 characters total are opened nearly 60 percent of the time. While subject lines above 70 characters also see a moderate standard open rate, for reasons that no one is quite sure of, subject lines that are between 60 and 70 characters are rarely if ever opened, even in an opt-in scenario like yours.

Additionally, it appears that subscriber based emails are more likely to generate a higher amount click throughs to the related website when the subject lines are longer and generating a large number of eyes on the page with shorter subject lines. This means that you can at least help prime the pump somewhat depending on the ultimate goal of each of your emails happens to be.

Don't underestimate the time you set to send your newsletter: Along similar lines as the subject line discussion, choosing the right time to send your newsletter can actually have a significant effect on both its open and click through rates. Studies show that people are going to be more likely to interact with your newsletter if they can read it early in the morning when they don't yet have to worry about the stressors of the day.

Emails sent during this time also have less ancillary email traffic to compete with, which also goes a long way towards a prospective customer taking more time to look through your offerings than they might otherwise, especially if they know you have a reputation for quality. This means an email sent after 8 pm will likely not be read until the next morning when people naturally factor in email time when starting their day. If you take the time of day you send your emails into account, you are likely to see as much as a 20 percent increase in both open and click through rate.

In addition to the time of day, the same ideas apply to the day of the week you ultimately decide to send your email. Studies show that emails sent Friday evening after 8 pm, Saturday and Sunday all have a statistically higher chance of being opened, with emails send Saturday gaining the biggest boost of an additional 25 percent chance of being open. This occurs for the same reason as above, there simply aren't that many people taking advantage of the off-peak hours and people have more free time which makes the more likely to interact with this type of content.

Give something away for free: Everyone loves getting something for nothing which is why people line up to have corporate logo t-shirts shot at them from a cannon. The same goes for the subscribers to your newsletter and if you routinely include digital products such as tools or templates or offer codes for real discounts (20 percent or better) on the products that relate to your newsletter this week, will go a long way to improving your interaction and click through rates. This is especially true early on when simply providing quality information might not be enough to get subscribers in the door and interested enough to open the email.

Don't underestimate mobile interaction: When it comes to reading emails, mobile solutions currently rank less than 5 percent behind more traditional email interaction methods. This means that if you ever hope to see the interaction and click through rates of your dreams you need to go out of your way to ensure that the mobile version of your newsletter is just as readily accessible as the more traditional model. Assuming that they will look at it later in the appropriate format is a surefire way to get your email deleted, sight, and site, unseen.

A few basic guidelines to consider in this arena include using a design template that is only a single column and making the font somewhat larger than what you would consider for a purely computer-based interaction. Additionally, you will want everything to be fully touch enabled and have buttons that are at least 44x44 when it comes to pixel width and height. Finally, it is important to keep in mind how a touch interface changes the interaction with the email and ensure that the content sticks to the middle of the screen to account for finger-based scrolling.

Keep your list active: Once you have built up your email subscriber list and operated your mailing list for a few months, you will want to reach out to inactive subscribers to show them home much more of an authority you have become in the interim period. In fact, studies show that the average mailing list is full of nearly 70 percent inactive participants; as such, reaching out to these users can bring a substantial number of subscribers back into the fold.

If you are reaching out to inactive subscribers it is important to include something especially enticing to convince them to open this email as opposed to all others. There is no magic bullet that will ensure all of your inactive subscribers return, which means reengaging will be all about experimenting in the space and determining what works most effectively for you, your business or website and your niche.

Ensure you are knowledgeable enough for the job

If you want to get the world to notice you and your online store or website to the point that they will consider you an authority on the niche in question then, aside from ensuring people will open your emails, you need to include the type of information people who are interested in your niche are likely to actually care about. To do this you need to know as much as a person can know about the niche in question.

Do your homework: The first thing to do is starting doing research, real research with books or academic websites, not blogs and not Wikipedia. A Wikipedia article is great for general information but that's not what you are looking for in this instance. You can start their sure, but only to look at the websites referenced at the bottom, start with those and go for there. There should be no piece of information or trivia that is too obscure for you to memorize. Take notes and refer to them frequently when you are creating your own content. The more information you can aggregate into your mind the better.

Be realistic: Remember, when it comes to gaining the right type of knowledge, you don't need to know everything about a general topic, sticking to the limits of your niche is perfectly acceptable; and even then, depending on your niche, being an authority in a subjection of it is perfectly respectable. The more focus you have the easier it will be to give yourself some breathing room and start chopping off related areas that are somewhat related to your focus, but not enough that you have to know everything about everything. Even universal names like Albert Einstein and Nikola Tesla had specialties, remember, a jack of all trades is a master of none.

Choose the right sub-niche: Depending on the niche in question, you might find that the current authority in the space is extremely entrenched to the point that you won't ever be able to dethrone them. If this is the case, then you simply are not drilling down deeply enough into the niche in question and you need to find an even narrow slice of the niche to become the authority in. If you are having trouble coming up with the right sub-niche, turning to Google might help.

To start, type the general niche that you are a part of into the search bar and then see what results autofill from there. While they might not be one-to-one results, what you see there can give you an idea of the types of things people care about in relation to the niche in question. No niche is so narrow that there isn't room for a second authority if you try hard enough. Think outside the box and you can create a space for yourself simply by being the first to view your niche in a specific way.

Write a guide: While you are still learning, you may find it helpful to write a guide to the topic that you are learning about. Not only could this be valuable content to use later, teaching will actually help you to become more comfortable with the material which will in turn make it easier to commit to your long term memory and also allow you to find new and improved ways of explaining both core and complicated concepts. Additionally, the formatting you use for this guide can be used to help outline future content, making it as clear and easy to understand as possible. Before you know it, you will have all of the information on the topic you could ever hope to need to know.

Don't stop until you can explain things in the common tongue: When it comes to learning everything about a specific topic, there are two levels of comprehension, the level that is enough to pass a test on the topic if you were taking a course on the subject, and the level of comprehension at which you can explain it to someone off of the street in a way that they understand it. Regardless of the niche that you are working in, you will know you have reached the appropriate level of knowledge when you can break down the complicated aspects of your niche in a way that your readers don't need to be experts to understand.

Most subscribers aren't going to open your newsletter for a regurgitation of simple facts, they will be opening your emails because they like the way you discuss the topic in question or the way you easily break down complicated topics. It is important to understand what unique spin you can put on the information in question, what your subscribers are looking for and what the niche as a whole is generally expecting. Mixing up these key factors is the way to ensure you are creating not just subscribers but followers.

Build relationships properly

Once you start sending out email blasts on the regular, it doesn't matter how much of an expert on a topic you are, word of your greatness will only spread if you take the time to build the proper relationships early on. You will want to nurture your early email list in the following ways to see the most surefire success.

Segment your list: As previously discussed, segmenting subscribers based on affiliations they create for themselves is a great way to ensure they start opening your emails, which is the first step to building any relationship. The more targeted your message is, the more likely you are going to convert a segmented follower to a general follower which is the point at which they start generating additional leads on their own.

Additionally, each of your segments should be personalized in such a way that it makes it clear to the subscriber that you are speaking to them directly in a way that is more than simply marketing speak. This means understanding the lingo of the niche you are representing and using a conspiratorial tone that indicates something about this segment is the segment that you really relate to the most. The more your subscribers feel as though they are opening an email directly from another person, the more likely they are to stick around long enough that they begin to view you as an authority.

Have a multi-tiered email approach: in addition to having a weekly or biweekly general newsletter, it is important to also utilize trigger emails at various points in the subscriber relationship to ensure they always feel connected to your store or site. These should include things like a welcome email as soon as someone joins the newsletter list explaining what to expect in the weeks and months ahead as well as the traditional outline of the average newsletter.

Additional trigger emails could include a variety of surveys to gain additional information or feedback as well as an email that is sent if someone stops opening emails for a prolonged period of time. As long as your emails don't devolve into spam, the more interactive the conversation you have with your subscribers the more likely they are to consider you an authority when it matters most.

Showcase your humanity: With automation taking over more and more of the functions that used to generate human interaction, taking the time to form a personal connection is the extra effort that you need to get subscribers to connect to you on a follower level. This means including your picture in every email and telling stories from your life, either real or fictional as long as they sound real, that emphasize all the ways that you and your subscribers are the same. Nothing seals the deal on a sale like a recommendation from a friend, especially a friend who is an authority in a given field.

Chapter 4

Intermediate Authority Building

Once you have the basics down, you will want to double down on the basis for authority that you have built so far. Layer in the following suggestions as you grow more confident with your audience and you will soon be the authority among your followers, if not necessarily the niche as a whole.

Hone your tone

While the type of content that you should be providing for your subscribers has already been discussed, how you present the information you are trying to convey is equally important when it comes to convincing your subscribers that you are one of them. This means that in addition to doing research on the hard facts of the niche in question, you need to get in the minds of your audience and speak like they speak, use the appropriate slang and know the right references. The best way to do this is to start by digging into the demographic data that you will have hopefully gathered by this point.

The first step is to start by picking out the key demographics related to your subscriber base and, if it appears to be those who are 30 or younger head to YouTube to see what tastemakers there have to say on the issue. If your niche is targeted at an older crowd, what you picked up in your studies should be enough to give you an idea of the tone your niche expects. For those with a younger niche, you will want to search for related terms on YouTube and watch content that is created by the content creators with the most amounts of views. Getting an idea of what these individuals sound like will help make your content seem more authentic and thus more authoritative because your subscribers will really feel it is coming from a peer.

With an idea of the type of language you will want to use, your next step should be to ask yourself how you want your subscribers to perceive you, aside from as an authority, and the action you want to push your subscribers towards. The more refined you can make your answer, the more effective you will find your future email newsletters to be. Additionally, you may find it helpful to think about the atmosphere, values and culture you are trying to project and the words and phrases that can make that as apparent to your subscribers as possible. There are many types of tone that can be effective depending on your overall goals, these include:

- *Informal:* An informal tone is a great tone to build towards, as long as you are careful to not roll it out to quickly as this is a tone that your readers are likely to feel that you have to earn, rather than adopting it without actually earning it. To maintain your authority with this tone it is important to strive to be enthusiastic and full of passion in regards to your niche and your need to share information; otherwise, you run the risk of coming off as unprofessional and thus lacking in authority.

- *Promotional:* It is important to rarely start newsletters with a promotional tone, at least until you have been sending out newsletters for long enough that your subscribers understand that it is the exception, not the rule. Likewise, it is important to maintain your authority throughout by giving very niche specific reasons as to the item you are selling is the best in its category, your favorite or just special for a reason that you felt the need to share.

- *Formal:* This is likely the tone you used for your first few email newsletters, but if you end up using it for too long, your subscribers won't feel as though they are having a conversation with a friend, they will feel like they are being lectured at. This is an easy tone to appear authoritative while using, but it is not the right type of authority that you should be striving to gain. Keep things fun and interesting and focus on insightful content to generate the proper type of authority instead.

- *Conversational:* This is likely the tone that you will find most useful when it comes to creating the types of email newsletters that do more than simply convey useful information. Making each newsletter feel as though it is part of a longer conversation that you are having with the reader can go a long way towards not only build a positive relationship but also towards creating a follower that will swear up and down that you have the most authority of everyone in the niche.

With the idea of the tone you are looking for firmly planted in your mind, the last thing you will want to do prior to sending out your newsletter each week is to check it for the following to ensure it is compelling as possible; remember, no one will stick around long enough to realize you are an expert if you don't make the extra effort to keep them interested. This means you should check the content for a natural rhythm, akin to that of a conversation, keep them engaged, be free of errors and always end with a call to action.

Find your voice

Regardless of what tone you end up using on the regular, it is important to strive to create your own unique voice that brings your personality, as well as the information you have learned, across in the words that you write. Remember, the information that you are putting forth is likely readily available from nearly any other expert in the niche you are striving to become the authority of. What will keep your subscribers opening your emails month after month and year after year is *you*. This is the time for everything that makes you unique to shine like you have never shined before.

While you will be able to get along just fine without having a unique voice at first, as your newsletter matures, you will begin losing open rates and click-throughs if you don't do something more to set yourself apart from all of the other content related to your niche. If you can't quite figure out what your voice is really all about, the following exercise may prove fruitful.

1. Start by picking three words that you feel best describe you. After you have picked them out, spend some time thinking about how you can best convey these characteristics in your writing. This can be by doing things like including asides, changing topics quickly or by using lots of examples or allusions.

2. Follow this up by considering how you naturally speak and how that can be conveyed in your writing. This can be conveyed in many ways, including in the way you structure your sentences and the way you vary the length of both your sentences and your paragraphs. Don't feel discouraged if you can't think of anything right away, a more robust understanding of your voice will come with time as long as you keep working at bringing it to the fore.

3. Write down a list of blogs that you read regularly, and if you don't read blogs on a regular basis, start now. The tone of a long-running blog is likely going to be the exact tone you are striving towards in your newsletters. Once you have an

idea of who you like and who you don't like, take it a step further and ask yourself what it is about the writing that you like the most. Picking out style choices that you like will make it easier to create your own style as a writer.

4. Think about your subscribers and the research you have done on them before considering how they would sound if you were speaking to them face to face. If you have the luxury of using YouTube or other influencers for research, then this should be easy to do. Otherwise, consider the types of references they are likely to have to make sense of the world around them and how they are likely to sound when they are speaking to their peers. Keep this frame of reference in mind and refrain from making references or assumptions that you don't think would track with your target audience.

5. Take an hour or so and just write about your day, your job, life in general, even what you see around you. The content doesn't matter, when you read it back to yourself, pick out specific instances where you feel like your voice is really coming through and then consider how you can expand that aspect and make it a larger part of your everyday writing. Again, it is important to not expect this to happen overnight, remember, slow and steady wins the race.

Once you have an idea of where you want to start, you will want to keep up that momentum by including more and more of your voice in your writing as time goes by. Don't be worried if at first you still can find the right words to express yourself in a way that is truly you, this will come with time and every email newsletter you write will make it easier to include a more fully formed voice for the next one.

Start a blog

If you haven't done so already, you need to create a section of your website, dedicated to providing the same type of information that you provide in your newsletter. Before you start a blog, it is important to understand that it is a substantial time commitment when done properly, though this will be somewhat mitigated at first as you will be able to reuse the topics that you have already covered in your newsletter. When putting your blog together it is important approach it in the appropriate context as when done correctly it can be a huge boost for the brand you are building and the authority behind it.

While having a quality email newsletter is an important way to build the idea of your authority with your subscribers, putting that information on your website is a good way to starting spreading that authority on a wider scale. What's more, once you are up and running on both fronts you can use the blog as a way of driving readers to subscribe to your newsletter by starting a post on your blog and then elaborating on it in your newsletter.

Have a strategy: Much like with your newsletter and your plan to build yourself up as an authority in your niche, you need to have a strategy when it comes to starting your blog and generating content for it regularly. The biggest part of your strategy should be related to how frequently you are going to be adding new content to the blog. A steady stream of new information will make your website look more professional, and thus more authoritative, but on the flipside, a blog that has a few posts and then sits fallow for months while you forget about it won't be doing you any favors and could even hurt your credibility with new visitors. This means you shouldn't expect to find the time to write your blog posts, you need to make the time, at least once or twice every week with one of those being continued in your newsletter.

Have a consistent voice: The voice of your newsletter is the voice that your subscribers have come to know and expect as you built your rapport with them over the opening salvo of your email newsletter experiment. It is important that the tone and voice that you use for your blog remains consistent with what your readers have already come to expect. A shift in tone can be jarring for readers and it can create a disconnect in the experience that you should avoid at all costs.

Cut your losses: If you find that, after giving it a try, blogging on the regular isn't working out, don't be afraid to deactivate the blog page from your website and go back to exclusive newsletter content. While this isn't recommended for the reasons outlined above, it is preferable to a blog that has gone stale or one whose content is not up to par with your brand in general. Remember, the goal is to improve your authority and a weak blog will do no such thing. Stick with your strengths and you are more likely to find the success you are looking for.

Show off your sources

While this is not something you need to make a habit of including in every newsletter you send out, from time to time it can be beneficial to your authority for your subscribers to get a more concrete idea of where your knowledge comes from. While it is natural to want to shy away from quoting other experts working in the same niche that you are working to prove your authority in. in reality quoting other experts and citing credible niche-related sources will make it clear to your subscribers that you really know what you are talking about because your information comes from such well-respected places.

The understanding that you value a credible source will help boost the level of trust that your subscribers feel for your content which, in turn, will make them more willing to accept other information that you put forth in the future. While it can be easy to make a commitment to only sharing content that is of the highest quality, finding this type of content can be easier said than done. As such, the following tips might make the process a little easier:

- Start by looking into the creator of the content in question to determine their level of authority in the field. If you have previously done your homework on your niche and you haven't heard of the person before, consider that a warning sign. Reliable sources should be easily verified with only a cursory Google search, if nothing shows up, then you should avoid the source entirely. The more connections to the niche, credentials and qualifications the author has, the better.

- Consider the author's affiliations, once you have determined that the author isn't just someone with a website and a lot of time on their hands, the next thing you will want to do is look into the associations, institutions or organizations they are currently affiliated with. Life is long, the person who created the content that you are trying to use could now be a very different person with very different hobbies and interests, some more frowned upon than others. You never know what you might find online, do the research for yourself or your subscribers will do it for you.

- Do some research and determining if the author of the content you are interested in using has any scholarly information that has been reviewed by peers in their field. This is a great place to look if the information being presented is beyond your level of knowledge and you want to ensure it is accurate before passing it on. If you can't find peered review work, it doesn't mean the information is not valid, as this is not a practice in all fields.

- Before you pass along any content it is important to check it for biases, even if it is likely that your subscribers share the same bias. An authority does not take sides; an authority makes decisions based on the inherent facts of the niche in question. If the content you are considering passing on includes blatant promotion or political or social messages, you cannot guarantee that the information you are sharing doesn't promote that agenda even if does not appear to on the surface.

- Consider how current the information is. Unless it relates to timeless truths related to your niche, the information you are passing along should be as fresh as possible. Passing along old information will make it appear as though you are out of touch with the current trends the niche may be experiencing.

- Check the sources that the information you are thinking about sharing provides. Depending on the source in question this may be completely normal or it can be seen as extremely out of the ordinary and a red flag the content may not be as legitimate as it first appears. When it comes to looking deeper into sources, you will also want to determine the relationship the author has with any sources that they cite as being experts on the topic.

- Consider the type of website that the information can be found on. If the information is found on a third party's personal website, then that information is going to be inherently more suspicious than if is coming through an official channel that is directly related to the niche in question. When it comes to determining the type of website that you are dealing with, it is important to avoid sourcing information form nonprofit organization websites as this information is almost always skewed towards the cause that the organization is promoting which will make it suspect in the eyes of your subscribers, suspicions you should share if you hope to be viewed as an authority when it comes to your niche.

- If you are not able to tell what type of website you are dealing with just by looking at the content you are interested in passing along, you may be able to find all the information you are looking for simply by checking the domain name associated with the information. The domain names .edu and .gov are likely always to provide information that can be sourced accurately, while some .org domain names can be related to reliable niche-based content, other are likely going to be biased and unusable. Some organizations with .edu domains do rent out space on their servers, however, so it is important to determine who owns the page as well as where it is hosted.

Chapter 5

Advanced Authority Building

Once you have gone out of your way to connect with your subscribers in a meaningful way, all that is left for you to do now is to seal the deal by following the remaining steps to maximizing your perceived authority in your niche of choice. Once you have established yourself as the dominant authority in your field, it will be important to keep up the good work and continue creating unique, insightful content regularly moving forward. Remember, being an authority is a marathon, not a sprint.

Expand your reach: While it will be easy for your subscribers to think of you as a credible source of valuable information by this point, if you hope to clear the last hurdle to true authority you will need to branch out. Your goal in this phase should be to spread out throughout the niche so that wherever your subscribers, and any other interested parties turn, they see your name and some useful content that you are talking about. This means forums related to the niche in question, the blogs of other experts in the niche, popular social media gatherings related to the niche, anywhere you can attach your name, you should try and be there twice. With enough exposure, your name will be directly associated with the niche by default through sheer force of will.

Additionally, when you post to these alternative venues, you will want to include your website as a part of your signature. By this point you should be confident in the content you are generating which means you know you are generating useful information which means you want to ensure that the people who want to find more of your insight know how to do so easily and with as little hassle as possible.

This goes double for guest posts on the websites of other experts, content syndication is also an option, consider bundling up a number of your previous newsletters and then reach out to other experts with websites and see if they would be interested in reposting your work. This will not only make their lives easier in terms of content creation, it will establish you as an authority in the niche to that expert's audience because of your broad reach.

Once you have reached out to a new audience, it is important to continue interacting with them in a way that will make them want to subscribe to your own newsletter as opposed to getting their information secondhand. This means creating an active social media presence and maintaining it in the long term. Just like a blog, having an active social media presence that reflects your authoritative status is important to looking professional and having a stale social media pages indicates that you are no longer on the top of your game.

While you can repost content from your newsletter as part of your social media presence, you need to really take advantage of the social aspect of the platform and make as many direct connections as you can make. It is one thing to be the type of authority that puts out decrees from an ivory tower, it is much more effective to be an authority that is seen as being out and amongst the people.

Become a published author

Remember the how-to guide you put together as a learning tool back when you were simply learning about your niche instead of teaching other everything there is to know about it? Hopefully you still have it handy as you can take what's there, add in some more information so that it is fully fleshed out and then publish it to the Amazon Kindle market for an automatic boost to your level of authority. Instead of being just someone who is talking about things online, you are suddenly a published author which holds weight even if the book is published digitally. What's more, you can then give away download codes for your book to all of your subscribers to ensure that you will have plenty of reviews to get things started on the right foot.

While it may seem difficult, in reality publishing a book has never been easier, especially if you are not overly concerned with the profits you make as a result. Publishing a book to the Kindle marketplace is completely free and Amazon then takes a percentage of each sale sold for the privilege. Likewise, if you already have the content prepped and ready to go, you can find someone to format your book and create a cover for it for only a few hundred dollars. There are also free programs online that can be easily found if you have the skills to create your book yourself making this authority-building activity practically free.

As an added bonus, you can then give copies of your book to the other experts in your niche and even if they don't talk about it much, a simple mention will be enough to establish your credibility in a wider circle, which is crucial if you ever hope to take the authority crown. Likewise, you will want to display the fact that you have written a book prominently on your blog so that it is the first thing new potential subscribers see when they look for more of your writing. Finally, you close the loop by offering a free copy of your book to those who sign up for your email newsletter where they can find more great content like what is readily available.

Make connections

By following through on these steps you should have made more connections with other experts in your niche, and if you wish to become the authority, then these are the people you are ultimately going to have to get on your side. This is a slow process, and one that is based almost entirely on the strength of the individual relationships that you form. To foster these relationships, you should start small, set up a regular spot as a guest contributor to their page, interact with them on social media and mention them by name when you talk to your followers.

Once they get word of your goodwill, they will likely reciprocate in kind, the online world is cutthroat and a little goodwill will go a long way towards seeing real results in the long term. At this point all you can do is to continue doing your research and producing the right types of content, after you build enough positive relationships you will find that other experts naturally start deferring to you when they are stumped, which you can bet their readers take note of.

Take your authority to the next level

By this point, if you are on track with all of the other suggestions listed in the last few chapters, then you should be well on your way to becoming the authority of note in your niche. To ensure that all of your various newsletters and blogposts don't lose focus over time, pepper in the following occasionally to keep people thinking about you and your authority in the proper way.

Advertise for the competition: **While obviously not the right choice all of the time, if you occasionally make it a point to recommend items that you don't even sell, then it will go a long way towards making the endorsement of products you do sell look more sincere by default. This plays on a basic standard of human psychology that makes others less distrustful when you lead with your weaknesses instead of your strengths because it appears you have less to hide. This in turn helps build a stronger relationship because your subscribers should feel as though you will always tell them the truth, even when it might not appear as though it is in your best interest.

Start talking about your hard work: If you have followed every suggestion up until this point then you know how much time and effort it has taken for you to proceed from being a member of the uneducated masses to the upmost authority in a given niche. It is time to start explaining what you have done to others as people tend to like stories of individuals who pulled themselves up by their bootstraps to find real success. Especially if you are already on a personal level with your subscribers, then it will give them the idea that they can follow in your footsteps.

Pull back on the sales talk: While you are likely quite used to including deals in your emails newsletters by this point, you might find that your sales improve if you start playing somewhat harder to get. If you make it clear that you are unwilling to compromise on anything, even your prices, you might find that the authority boost this stance commands can be enough to make up the difference in customers who prefer sales prices. Additionally, you will find that more of your followers are likely to purchase items that you discuss in terms of real world usage scenarios then other, more sales oriented pitches. A higher level of confidence indicates your authority and makes followers more likely to do what you say.

Upgrade your newsletter

While a simple email newsletter is appropriate for a time, as word of your authority grows, so will the expectations related to the content you create. This means that eventually you will want to up your newsletter related game and try HTML email newsletters instead. When it comes to understanding HTML email, it is important to realize that it is more than attaching some code and images to a blank email and clicking send. This is because the image links are typically going to break in this scenario, sending all of your hard work into the either and making you look less professional, and thereby less authoritative in the process. Additionally, if you send the code in the traditional fashion, it won't generate anything more than a string of code for your subscribers to ponder over.

Instead, you will need to include the email in what is known as MIME format which will allow the utilized code to be sent to your subscribers, along with a plain-text version in case the HTML doesn't render properly. This process can be rather complicated if you aren't extremely familiar with coding which is why it is recommended that you look into an email platform or program that does a lot of that type of heavy lifting for you.

When it comes to determining what type of design you want to use to take advantage of your new and improved email newsletter approach, the first thing you should keep in mind is that when it comes to keeping a modern design aesthetic, less is more. The added design should complement the style of your website, but also the tone of your content that your subscribers have come to expect. All told, you never want a layout that has a width more than 600 pixels as doing so will make it difficult for many email clients to see the images without taking additional steps to do so.

Once you have designed your new and improved email newsletter template, it is important to test your designs before you send them live to all of your subscribers. While mistakes happen, the closer to perfect you can appear to your subscribers the more likely they are to put all of their niche related faith in your authority. This means you will want to test your template across as many different usage cases and email clients as possible.

It is important to understand that some clients will remove tags from your content, while others won't support flash and others still block all pictures by default. While you likely won't ever be able to account for all of the different things that have the potential to go wrong, if you send your new sample to a reasonably sized test audience you should be able to account for many of the potential errors. Regardless, you should have safeguards in place to ensure your subscribers will be able to see your content, even if they can't see your template.

Start creating scarcity

While you should be sure to continue giving your subscribers plenty of freebies just for being swell and supporting you, you should also begin offering certain things that are only available in limited quantities. People naturally want what they can't have which means that if they suddenly can't get a hold of your content then they will naturally start to value it even more than they did before.

There are three primary types of scarcity, the first is where you tell your subscribers that only a specific number of individuals are going to get access to something special if they do a specific thing. This is beneficial because it can show you just how popular you are among your subscribers and also because it can lead to additional instances of the action before people realize the limited number has expired. The second type of scarcity is when you offer something for a limited period of time such as a 24-hour deal. Finally, the last type of scarcity has to do with making it seem as though you have far more subscribers than you can handle in terms of the content which is why subscribers should hurry to take advantage while they can.

Look the part

If you are planning to be the authority in a given niche you will need to give in to the general conception of what a person who is an expert in that niche looks like. This could mean dressing professionally by always being well-groomed and in a suit for pictures, or it could mean growing out your hair, throwing away your suit and buying a pair of cigarette leg jeans. Whatever it is, you will always appear to be on the fringe of the niche until you embrace it fully and look the part in all of your pictures and whenever you meet a subscriber in public. Remember, you are as much a part of your brand as the content you create, every photo is an opportunity to show that you bleed the niche in question as only a true authority would.

Stand for something

Regardless of the niche in question, there is always a dividing issue that everyone comes down on either side of. This can be a long standing debate or something that is happening in the moment in your community, but whatever it is, you need to come out in regards to the issue and prove to your followers that you are more than just a talking head, you are a true leader of the community. It is important to not come out in favor of an issue in the moment, however, and to do your research and ensure you are on the appropriate side. Nothing can kill a potential authority faster than coming down on the side of an issue that turned out to be several misinformed. Be considerate, but also be decisive and the niche should rally around your fortitude.

Chapter 6: Tips for Improving Your Metrics

If you feel that you have done everything in your power to become a true authority in your field but it still seems as though your success metrics aren't where you would like them to be, then it may be time to revisit your open rate, click through rate, conversion by source and forward rate strategies.

Open Rate

If your open rate has never been where you want it, or it started out great and has since dropped off, then it may be time to rethink your subject line strategy. In fact, studies show that stale email newsletters can see open rates improve by as much as 50 percent simply by changing up their expected subject line habits. To help you get started, look no further than the plethora of list-based articles and their grabbing headlines. Consider subject lines that start with leading lines such as:

- There's no way you'll believe this…
- The – everyone is talking about…
- You won't believe how easy it is to…
- You have to see it to believe it…

While they might sound corny, it may be just the boost to your standard routine to start seeing the types of results you are looking for. You can also use strange or clever subject lines, though they are likely to lose effectiveness if used on the regular. Regardless, it is important to prune your email list every 6 months to ensure you are tracking the right data.

Click through rate

If you feel that enough of your subscribers are routinely opening your emails and taking advantage of your content but you just don't seem to see a click through rate that supports your open rate, then the first thing you should consider the true root of the problem. This means the best place to start is to include some serious deals on a few common products, deals that are literally too good to miss, in your next email newsletter.

If the click-through rates on these deals are significantly more robust than normal, then you may simply need to start offering more attractive deals in order to make the click through rate worth your time. Alternatively, if you still find your click through rate low though your open rate remains acceptable then you may need to consider finding ways to ensure customers are reading to the end of each newsletter.

The simplest way to do this may be to simply cut back on the amount of content that you are including in each of your newsletters as there might simply be too much clutter on the page to lead to the type of results that you are looking for. Strip things back a little and see if your results improve as it is important to not become so focused on being the best that you lose track of improving your sales which is what all of this authority building has been for. Once you cut back on your content you can then begin adding more back in until you find the right balance.

Conversions by source

If, despite your authority in your niche you find that your conversions by source aren't where you would like them to be, then there are a few things you will want to ensure you are doing properly before moving on to more advanced tactics. The first thing you will want to consider is the HTML email you are using.

If it is comprised of one large picture, then if that picture can't be displayed for any reason then you are cutting out a large portion of your customer base. Go back to the testing phase and ensure everything is working in as many different scenarios as possible and see if things improve.

Additionally, your conversions might be down because you are offering up too many choices and your subscribers are experiencing choice paralysis. Especially as your focused has shifted from just an email newsletter to a blog and being seen as an authority in the niche as a whole it is natural for your newsletter to pick up bloat along the way. Slice and dice, shake it up and maybe try something new, your conversions could simply be down because fatigue has set in. You may even want to stop publishing a newsletter for a short period of time, just so people can realize they miss your expertise. Then, when you come back new and improved, your conversion rate should naturally jump as a result.

Forward rate

Even if your other metrics are looking good, getting your forward rate to rise regularly can be a difficult nut to crack. As previously mentioned, if your email newsletter has picked up some bloat as time has passed then it likely reaches a much broader audience as well.

Unfortunately, studies show that mass appeal is the enemy of the forwarded email and the more focused an email newsletter is on a specific topic or issue, the more likely it is for subscribers to forward that email to other interested parties. Along those same lines, subscribers are more likely to pass along your email newsletters to members of the same niche if they feel you are expressing targeting them with interesting information. Again, it may be time to reassess the entire focus of your email newsletter and reformat it to get it back to its original intention.

Perhaps unsurprisingly, that same study found that the number one best way to get your followers to share your email newsletters is to simply ask them to do so. By including a call to action to share the email with a friend, even if you include other social media options, followers are much more likely to forward the email to at least one friend. While this may seem surprising, it really shouldn't be. By this point your followers likely think of you as one of their friends, and anyone would be willing to do something as simple as forwarding an email for a friend.

Chapter 7

Popular Email Marketing Platforms

While the type of content and your perception as an authority are going to go a long way towards whether or not your subscribers stick around for the long term, at least part of the subscriber retention process rests on the platform you use for all your email marketing needs which is why the following list has been complied, specifically with small businesses in mind.

Mail Chimp

This long running service offers up all of the tools that you could need to establish your email newsletter and grow it into an email blast that contains tens of thousands of users. The platform is also easily customizable without any programing skills which makes it great for those with more business sense than programing sense. Mail Chimp includes many of the most common features including a variety of templates, automatic segmentation options including geolocation, plenty of social media integration, the ability to generate surveys, full Google Analytics integration and the ability to generate permalinks for each email.

Mail Chimp offers both free and paid services with the free option allowing for a maximum of 2,000 subscribers total and the ability to generate a total of 12,000 unique emails each month. This is plenty for those who are just starting out and still looking to build a solid subscriber base. The paid version of the software starts at $15 per month and scales from there based on the number of subscribers in the mailing list.

Constant Contact

If you already own an existing small business in the real world and are interested in being more active in the online space, then Constant Contact may offer up the feature set that you are looking for. It offers a wide variety of options when it comes to manage segmented lists, a feature which looks for and removes duplicate email address, integration with numerous other applications including all the major social media players and easy drag and drop email editing options. What's more, it offers up an elaborate set of tools for those who get stuck in the process including tutorials, videos, FAQs, chat email and live phone support.

Constant Contact is most likely not the choice for advanced users as it lacks some of the customization that power users would appreciate as well as any autoresponder technology. Constant Contact offers users a 30-day free trial and after that their plans start at $15 per month for email lists with 500 contacts or less and scales from there to $150 each month for a list with 25,000 contacts. If you are running a nonprofit organization take note, you can get a discount with Constant Contact.

EMMA

EMMA is perhaps the email platform with the most modern design aesthetic and a hassle free management system to match. It offers detailed customization options outside of the traditional segmentation choices, automated emails including autoresponders, free image hosting, a modern interface, drag and drop designs and plenty of form and survey options as well. They offer a focus on the automated side of things with new and eye catching designs for their templates. They also offer an express focus on mobile-based templates that all come with Google Analytics tools baked in.

Unfortunately, EMMA currently doesn't offer any way to report spam emails or to test via an A/B split. They don't have any free offerings, though for $35 per month they offer plans that fit 1,000 subscribers.

Aweber

Aweber was one of the first email marketing platforms on the scene which means it offers all of the features you expect in the easiest to use interface time and experience can manage. The consistency and deliverability of the company that practically invented the email marketing platform is also top notch while still being simple enough that those who are not technically savvy can use comfortably. Additionally, Aweber offers split testing, autoresonders, segmentation options, personalization options, person-to-person support services, subscriber tracking, and in-depth and detailed personalization options.

Unfortunately, Aweber does not currently offer any Google Analytics functionality or survey features. Aweber services start at $20 each month for up to 500 subscribers and up to $150 for anywhere from 10,000 to 25,000 subscribers.

IContact

When it comes to easy to use interfaces, IContact might be the easiest of them all. This is because even though the feature set is as robust as many of its competitors, it keeps the interface simple at every step. IContact features include full-service support, layout optimization options, consistent delivery rate, plenty of automated options, testing for A/B splits, segmentation options, CMS options, contact management features and social media support. IContact starts at $10 per month for lists with 250 subscribers and increases to $110 each month for 15,000 subscribers.

Conclusion

Thank for making it through to the end of *Email Marketing: Strategies to Capture and Engage Your Audience, While Quickly Building an Authority*, let's hope it was informative and was able to provide you with all of the tools you need to achieve your goals both in the near term and for the months and years ahead. Remember, just because you've finished this book doesn't mean there is nothing left to learn on the topic. Becoming an expert at something is a marathon, not a sprint, slow and steady wins the race.

The next step is to stop reading already and to start working out the ways you are going to work to actively create your own aura of authority in your chosen niche in both the short and the long term. While it may first feel as though the path to expert, much less authority is endlessly long and continuously uphill, it is important to keep in mind it will get easier the longer you keep it up. Becoming an authority isn't a short process and if you want to reap the rewards you have to put in the time, day after day and email after email; however, if you keep it up the results can be substaintial.

Finally, if you found this book useful in anyway, a review on Amazon is always appreciated!

Email Marketing:

Tips and Tricks to Increase Credibility

Table of Contents

Introduction 141

Chapter 1:Gaining the Trust of Others................................... 143

Chapter 2: Starting your Email List... 149

Chapter 3: Tips to Build Credibility Through the Computer...... 151

Chapter 4: Writing your Brochure... 157

Chapter 5: Welcome Emails... 161

Chapter 6: Tips for all your Emails.. 165

Chapter 7: Recurring Emails.. 173

Chapter 8: Editing Your Email 181

Chapter 9:Your Subject Line.. 187

Chapter 10: Selling in Your Email 193

Chapter 11: Ways to Get Email Addresses 197

Chapter 12- Building Your Credibility Some More 199

Conclusion.. 201

Introduction

I want to thank you and congratulate you for purchasing the book, *"Email Marketing Tips and Tricks To Increase Credibility"*.

This book contains proven steps on how to increase your credibility through email marketing.

If you own a business or just want to sell more product, these tips and tricks will grow your client base and multiply your sales. These are easy techniques to improve your emails and your reputation.

Thanks again for purchasing this book, I hope you enjoy it!

Chapter 1

Gaining the Trust of Others

Building credibility starts with you. Even before you put your fingers on a keyboard, you must have made decisions about yourself and your company or product.

Credibility is being trusted. Being trusted starts with values. Write down the values that you will not budge on. Those values that you will defend in all cases. Do not write down values that you do not truly believe in. It is extremely important that you be honest with yourself in this step of the process. If you are not sincere it will come through to your clients, customers, and friends and they will not feel that you are trustworthy. Consider writing a mission statement for yourself. A mission statement can give your company a purpose besides money. It allows you to have a clear cut idea of what it is you consider to be most important about your business. In the future your mission statement could promote your business by being a prime example of your beliefs and telling clients that they can trust you. Try writing down some of your values and possibly a mission statement right now. Here are some examples of how values could affect your business goals. Below are some value based intentions.

- Precipitate positive change in the world.
- Resolve all types of issues whether they be within the company or in the local state.
- Be a moral agency.

- Generate enthusiasm in employees and clients.

- Make things happen. Have a positive outlook and expect that you can make anything happen that you set your mind to.

Standards are a bit different from your beliefs and values. Your standards are the way your company should be run to make money and satisfy your customers. Some categories of standards could be:

- Customer service- How you treat your clients.

- Transactions- The amount of time purchases take or the way that they are handled.

- Handling of currency- The protocol you follow in case of theft, where you store money, and who is allowed to handle the money.

- Client demands- The requests of your customers.

- Marketing- The way you advertise your company.

- Organization tasks- The ins and outs of the duties associated with your business day to day.

Here are some examples of some principles you may or may not hold for yourself:

- Customer service: You may make a promise to yourself that whether someone buys from you or doesn't you always want them to leave smiling. Always address your clients in a polite manner. Let customers know how long the product will take to arrive and if there are any issues in the process, inform them immediately. Respond to online inquiries within 2 days.

- Client demands: Do everything in your power to grant the wishes of the customer, even if it requires extra hours of work on your part.

- Transaction Time: This could be, for example, 24 hours maximum amount of time needed to conduct the purchase.

- Call protocol- Respond to all calls as quickly as possible. When it is the wrong number, do your best to direct the customer to the correct employee. Remain on the phone until the customer has hung up.

- Co-Worker Behavior- Be respectful to each other. Have weekly meetings to keep everyone updated on current project deadlines. Be amicable with all other employees in order to guarantee satisfaction in the workplace.

Once you have written down your values, standards, and principles and been honest with yourself about them, you can move on to figuring out who you are. What is your personality? Are you a straightforward person or more of a joker? Do you like to talk or would you rather listen? You need to know the answers to these questions so that when you are in the midst of talking to someone or writing an email you can be sure you are exemplifying to them exactly who you are, being genuine, and not being a fraud. People these days see everything as black and white. You are either trustworthy or not. If they get the feeling that you are not being true to you then they will feel lied to and you have lost your credibility already. You can decide which of these personality traits you may have and of course add your own:

- Adventurous- Fearless, bold

- Calm- relaxed, quiet, not easily angered

- Flexible- easygoing

- Logical- rational, reasonable
- Optimistic- Thinking positive thoughts first
- Passionate- Excited and intense
- Realistic- practical
- Sympathetic- Able to understand and be sensitive of someone else's feelings.
- Witty- Funny

After you have made it very clear to yourself who you are then you must make sure you know your product or company inside and out. You need to know every single thing there is to know. Write down some questions about your product that you may encounter. Ask friends and family what questions they may ask if they were being targeted by this company. Then write down your answers. If you do not know the answer, find out. You do not want to be asked a simple question about your product and not know what to say. This takes your credibility away. The customer will want to know that he is in good hands working with you. He wants to know that you know your product. If you do not know your product, how could you possibly believe in it? The more questions you answer, the more comfortable people will feel around you and the more confident you will feel. Clients like a confident salesperson. Here are some questions you can answer about your product:

- What are your personal experiences with this product or service?
- What is the point of the commodity?
- How would you characterize it? What does it look like, feel like, smell like?

- How can they obtain it? Is it delivered or do they pick it up in store?

- What is the price? Do they have to do anything else before receiving it?

- Why should they get it from you and not someone else?

What are the attributes of your product and why is it advantageous for your clients to use it? Below are some examples of questions about the attributes and a possible advantage.

- What is the benefit in using your commodity? It will cut down on wasted time.

- How does it operate? It is uncomplicated and can be used by anyone.

- How is it generated? It is not harmful to the environment in the process of producing it and is recyclable after being used.

Next, decide who your target audience will be. Your tone is dictated not only by who you are but who you are talking to. If you are targeting moms it is clear that you will want to make it sound as if your product is in the best interest of her family because that is what is most important to her. If you are selling to busy businessmen however, you will want to sell the fact that the company will never waste any of their time. If you are not sure who your target audience would be, take into account who your current clients are. What type of needs do they have? What keeps them up at night? What are their day to day problems? Where do they spend time? What do they buy regularly? What is it about your company that makes their lives better or easier? What do they dislike about companies? What do they dislike about people? The answers to these questions will help you figure out exactly who to target and how to do so. You will want your company to somehow meet their needs, help them sleep at night, solve their problems. You will want to market your company where they spend time regularly, the places they shop. Tell them how your company has made lives just like theirs better already. Stay away from the things they dislike about companies. Stay trustworthy by being exactly what they expect and want in a business.

In more general terms you may want to decide whether you market primarily to men or women? What age group purchases your product? Are they married? What do they do for a living? On the other hand, if you are looking to sell to a company, how many people work at the company? What service or product does that company offer?

Once you have answered all these questions about who you are, your values, your products, and your clients then you will finally be ready to start your email marketing. All this information will keep your credibility high as you sell your product through your emails and to your wonderful clients.

Chapter 2

Starting your Email List

So now you know everything there is to know about yourself, your product and your potential clients but how do you get the email addresses for these potential clients? You never want to send an email without specific permission. Spam emails are bad for business, they make you look untrustworthy and dishonest. Here are some ways you can collect email addresses while keeping your credibility intact.

- Have a sign-up sheet at a physical location. A small flyer with a description of what your emails will contain and a spot to add your email is a good old fashioned way to build on your email list. You can have these at booths or just stores that allow marketing flyers.

- Include a way to sign up for your email list via your website. If a client frequents your website, chances are they will have no problem receiving emails from you as well.

- If you send products to homes in packages, include a flyer on how to join your email list. A fan of your product is likely a fan of your emails.

- Use your social media outlets such as Facebook to post clear instructions on how to sign up to receive emails.

- Motivate your employees to gather email addresses by offering them special rewards when they get a certain number.

Email Marketing

- Ask your loyal customers to tell their friends about you. You can even offer them incentives as well.

Starting your email list is a very important step before actually writing an email so make sure you do so before trying to send any content.

Chapter 3

Tips to Build Credibility Through the Computer

You have your email list ready and want to build your rapport and credibility. Here are a few tips to exude integrity and trustworthiness through the computer.

- Answer all your emails in a timely manner. If you can, have your emails come through to your cell phone so that you can answer them all hours of the day. Receiving a prompt response is extremely important to clients. One of the most frustrating things you can do is be slow to respond or not respond at all. Your clients will truly appreciate a quick reply. Even if you are not quite able to answer their question yet, if you can email back and tell them you will have an answer for them by morning, it will make all the difference. You can take your own experiences into consideration with this one. Think back to emails that you have sent to coworkers or other companies. How did you feel when you did not receive a response for days? On the other hand, what did you think when you were sent an answer within minutes? Quick replies will build your rapport with your client.

- If there is anything about your product that can go wrong in certain situations or if it does not fit the needs of some people, be honest about it. This will build credibility and the purchase may very well still go through if the positives outweigh the negatives. If, however, someone were to buy it without knowing the negatives, this would hurt your reputation with not just the one client but everyone he talks to. Even if they do not buy it, for example if it is simply not made for them, they might still recommend it to someone that would be better fit for it. They would do this because you were honest and they have no negative feelings toward you.

- Follow through with your clients. When you have conversations about the business or certain products with clients and then stop hearing from them for a bit, do not give up on them. An email to ask if they are still interested, about a week after they stopped answering may remind to seal the deal. Even clients who are not necessarily ready to buy anything should receive a follow up email. Ask them how they are doing and if they might have any questions for you. Let them know that you are available at any time to help them with a purchase. Just be there for them and make sure they know you are there.

- Always follow through with your promises. When you tell them you will email them back with a new offer tomorrow, make sure that you do. Following through on promises is the age old secret to building lasting and trusting relationships.

- Give them more than they expect. If they know you work from nine in the morning to five in the evening, do not hesitate to answer their email after dinner. When they order a product from you, throw in something small just as a thank you. Send them emails to thank them for their business and birthday emails on their special day. The fact that you go above and beyond will resonate with them very strongly.

- Keep all your customers information confidential. Every single piece of information that they give you including simple things like their age or weight must be a secret between you and your client. Even if they did not specifically ask for you to keep their information confidential, everything that is said over email should always be private.

- Ask for feedback from your clients as well as your coworkers. If you have a reputation of taking criticism appropriately and changing your business practice based on client needs, you will seem open minded and easy to work with. The fact that you didn't just take the criticism but actually asked for it will make the customer feel that his opinion matters to you, especially if you change your ways based on what they tell you.

- Respect your client's schedule. If they tell you they cannot purchase the product until next month, do not pester them about it before then. Set a schedule with them early on of when the best times to contact them are. If they know you care enough to only contact them at the times they told you, they will feel like you really pay attention and put their needs first.

- Do everything in your power to make their life a little easier. If they need something the very next day, can you overnight ship it? If the product broke before a deadline, can you send them a new one as fast as possible? They are your priority, make sure they know that.

- When you first start working with someone, have them define for you what they hope to get out of the business relationship. Ask them to define for you the pros and cons that they feel about working with you. This will help you decide which products or services will be most helpful to them and it will allow you to focus on their needs and not try to push unwanted items on them. It will also allow you to realize what their fears are about working with you and keep you from becoming unwanted.

- When you are getting to know your client and asking them questions, ask more questions based on the answers. This will prove to them that you are paying attention to their answers and that you care about their life.

- When you are asked questions, give clear answers. Do not be vague. Vague answers mean that you are not sure what the client wants to hear and are trying to please them no matter what. A definitive answer will build trust.

- Explain anything that your client may be confused about. You don't ever want the customer to be unsure of anything.

- Stay in touch with the fact that your client is changing. Everyone is always changing so make sure you are aware of your customers' needs at all times.

- Respond to your clients requests and emails by paraphrasing their comments. This will not only prove you were paying attention to what they were saying but it will also make sure that you understand them correctly.

- Make sure you regularly email your repeat customers. Just let them know that you are around if they need anything. You must care for your relationships even when they are not in the process of using your services.

- Show your client you care about what they are feeling. Put yourself in their shoes and prove to them that you did. If they are upset that their product did not arrive on time,

Email Marketing

apologize to them and tell them, for example "I see how it would be very inconvenient to have to hold the meeting when you had not yet received the conference phone." Showing them that you can empathize is critical to a real relationship.

- Try to gauge what information your client may need before they even ask for it. The more you can answer questions before they are asked, the more they will feel comfortable with you and perceive that you know them well.

- Stay unbiased. Even though it may seem that you should be biased toward your product, when speaking to your client, this is not true. You want your client to feel that you have their concerns in mind. You are willing to send them to a different company if it turns out someone else would be best suited to help them. If a client can sense this from you, they will trust you more and are more likely to listen to your advice on what to purchase.

- Never assume that they received your email. You don't want your client to miss important information because you assumed incorrectly. If you did not get a response, resend it with a note that says you just wanted to make sure they got it. Sometimes emails are sent to spam for unknown reasons. Never put the blame on a client. The most important thing is just to know that they received it in the end and move on.

- Sharing information about yourself allows your client to feel like they are getting to know you. As important as it is for you to ask the client questions and make them feel like you want to know them, they also want to know you. No one wants to buy from a stranger. Send your clients a professional picture of yourself with a paragraph that includes your age, information about your family, your favorite things to do and most importantly why you love working for your company.

- Be active on social media. Try to answer questions and post comments as often as possible on Facebook and Instagram. The more people see your opinions and fact based messages on the internet, the more they feel like they know you. People love to follow famous people on social media because it makes them feel as if they know this person. Make yourself known through these channels. If you have employees, encourage them to be active as well. The more people are talking about or just representing your company, the better.

Gaining the trust of others can be hard but by following these tips you ensure your very best chance at others seeing you as a credible source for purchasing products or services.

Chapter 4

Writing your Brochure

Now you are ready to sit down and write an email. There are several types of marketing emails. There are regular weekly or monthly emails, "Here is a bargain!" emails and "Welcome to the email list" emails. You can also send brochure emails to someone who specifically asked about a certain product.

You need to be able to hand the potential clients some brochures. Answering questions about your product builds credibility but so does being prepared and time management is important to both you and your client. These examples also work for a marketing email. If someone asks you for information about your product you can just as easily write down their email address and send them an email brochure. This is great because it is not as easily lost as a paper brochure and it also allows you to invite them to your email list.

Here is some information on what to include in a brochure email:

- Your website or any online reviews from others.
- Testimonials
- Three to five advantages of using your product
- Some sort of discount such as a voucher or coupon.
- Pictures that relate to your product or service. These photos should be both to make your brochure more

Email Marketing

appealing as well as to demonstrate the advantages of your product.

Here is some more information on writing an email brochure:

- Be precise about what you are selling with this brochure. Do not make the brochure for all of your products or your whole company. Make it about one specific service you offer or the product that your client was curious about. The brochure is a selling point and you cannot sell all your products in one email. The more detailed you are about one product or service the more potential there is for interest from the receiving end.

- Keep your word count low. The faster someone can read through and learn about your product, the better. If they are emailed a brochure with a lot of text, there is a high likelihood that they immediately move on to the next email. Time is very important to everyone. Keep this in mind when typing out your brochure.

- Use bullet points to highlight very specific sections of your brochure. This way when your client has a question, they know which section to jump to and read about. It also makes it more easily read. It makes more text feel like less, allowing you room to add more advantages without making them feel overwhelmed with text.

- Make sure the brochure is specific to the person reading it. Remember who your target audience is and only add the advantages that are most likely to influence this buyer. Also add pictures that are eye catching for that type of person, whether it be organized and clear cut or more chaotic and artsy.

- Do not include irrelevant information. As much as you want to show off about how many were sold worldwide, this information can be used in a later email. Make sure the brochure that is highlighting this product is doing only that. This will keep it shorter and also more interesting therefore more readable.

- The words and pictures should complement each other. Have you seen those paper brochures that have a beautiful picture on the front with just enough words to get you interested? This way you open the brochure and this is when you see the rest of the information. That is what you want the beginning of your email to feel like. For example if you had a dating website you could have the words "Are you looking for your perfect match?" at the top of the email with a great picture of a couple getting married. If they truly are interested in a dating website, they will immediately move on the rest of the email. Now they are hooked because their answer to your question was yes.

- Give examples of real world situations where your product worked wonderfully. If you have permission, use names of some of your clients and quote them directly. You can have your testimonials with added examples of exactly how your product was helpful to them. Sometimes when your clients give you quotes for brochures, they only say that they loved it for this or that reason but do not have their story written out. With their permission you can have their testimonial next to their story which you have typed up yourself. Since you sold them their product and know why and how they used it, it should be no problem for you to write this down on paper.

- At the end of your email style brochure, tell them exactly what they need to do next and how. This way there is no confusion or leaving it for later.

A brochure is a great quick way to make sure the client gets as much information as possible about the product he is interested in while also creating an email connection that allows for back and forth emails in the future.

Chapter 5

Welcome Emails

It is very important that you send welcome emails to new or potential clients that have trusted you with their email addresses. When you send the first email you should make sure it actually makes you feel welcome, after all it is called that for a good reason.

- Send the welcome email within 24 hours of them giving you their information. It is important to send it while they still remember you and you are at the top of their mind. If you wait too long, they may have forgotten you and will delete the email thinking it is just spam even though in reality they had handed you their email address themselves.

- In your welcome email, make sure you have an about you. This is a good way for the client to learn exactly what kind of company they are receiving emails from and decide whether they want to stay on your email list. It is a good place to gain some credibility through introducing yourself as the respectful, honest person that you are. When writing an about you page, tell your professional story. Let them know how you got to be working for this company and why it is that you are so happy you do. Tell them what you can do for them. Even though it is an "About you" section, you still want to make it clear that they are your first priority. Give examples of how you have helped others in similar situations as them. The last and most important thing is to make it clear to them why they can trust you.

- Make sure you tell them why it was a great idea for them to join the email list. Is it because they will now receive coupons or because they will be updated on the stores holiday closings? Will you always include an inspirational quote for those days that they may just feel like they need that extra motivation?

- Adding a coupon or promotion to the very first email is a great way of making them feel like they made the right decision in giving you their email address. They will automatically feel rewarded for their actions and your credibility will increase a little bit.

- If possible have a "shop now" button directing them to your website and your products. They just signed up for your list so chances are they are excited about your products right now and this is the best time to get them acquainted with what you have to offer.

- Adding pictures to your first email will make it a warmer welcome. If you are a service-based company, a picture of your team will do just fine. If on the other hand you have some product to show off, go ahead and draw attention to that great merchandise.

- Make sure your email works on cell phones. A mobile friendly welcome email is extremely important, especially in a world where so many people now check their mail on their cell phones.

- You can add a link to your website, to make it easy for them to check out your online presence but make sure you do not go link crazy. One or two links maximum are best, otherwise they won't click on any of them from the sheer intimidation of all the choices.

- A welcome email of all emails should be signed with a person's name instead of a company name. This is friendlier and lets them know someone specific wants to take care of their purchases. As always, this is just another way to add to your credibility a bit.

- You may want to let them know exactly what types of emails you will be sending their way in the future. This way they feel like they know exactly what they signed up for and can decide whether that is really what they wanted.

- In the unlikely event that they want to unsubscribe, make sure you have a clear button for them to do so. This is a very good way to build credibility. No one wants to lose customers from their email list but allowing them to do so whenever they may want, makes your company more trustworthy. Also have an email confirming their addition to the email list. This way you know for sure you don't have anyone marking you as spam. If they clearly know they signed up, they will be eagerly awaiting your emails. The confirmation email will let them know that you don't plan on ever sending them anything they do not ask for and in turn will make them trust you more.

- If you have social media, create a link from the welcome email to show them how to become a fan on Facebook or follow you on twitter. Social media goes hand in hand with emails. It is all part of the wonderful online world of marketing. If your client has just decided to receive emails from you, chances are they are happy to add you to their instagram as well.

Your customer should feel welcome from the very first email you send them. This is creating a connection that will grow through your following emails. This is extremely important because it counts as the first point of email contact.

Chapter 6

Tips for all your Emails

A welcome email is extremely important but so is every other email afterward, especially since they can click the unsubscribe button at any point.

Below are some tips to follow with every marketing email.

- The first and most important thing is be a friend. That's right. Would you rather open an email from the grocery store or from your long lost high school best friend? Your friend of course! So be a friend. Make sure that every time someone sees an email come in from you they want to open it. You want them to feel that the email was specifically written just for them even though it is actually being sent to your entire email list. Personalizing it is not the right touch. Many times companies put your name in specific spots in the email so as to make it look like it is just for you but actually a lot of the time it just makes it feel more robotic. Think about it. The email is repeating your name multiple times per paragraph. Do you do that when you are talking to your friend? No? Then do not do it to your client. You must remember that your client is your friend. If it were not for your clients, you would have no company.

- Friends do not email on cue. They email when they have something to say. Every email you send should have a purpose. Do not send emails just for repetition. The more emails people see from you in their inbox the more they

Email Marketing

feel spammed which then lands you in the spam filter with less people reading your email.

- **Friends are helpful.** Make sure that every time you send out an email, you add something to the text which is somehow helpful to the reader. If it is just an inspirational quote, so be it. You want your reader to have a reason to open your email every week. If he knows that every time he reads your mail he feels a little better afterward or gets something out of it then he will absolutely stop his day for the five minutes it takes to read your mail. Again though, do not send mail every day, even if it does have something helpful in it. There is such a thing as too helpful and clients will no longer look forward to your email no matter what the content, if the email is sent too often.

- **Friends tell the truth.** Your credibility is easily lost when you lie. You must make it clear to the client exactly what your emails consist of even before you send them. If you send emails every week, make sure they know that. If you tell them that they won't receive but one email and then they receive one every week they will automatically put you in the spam filter without even reading your email. It is very important to always tell the truth about both what the emails will contain and the actual contents. Do not promise anything you cannot deliver. Your credibility will grow every time the reader feels he was treated the right way. It is respectful to tell them exactly the truth. Lying by omission will still feel like a lie to a client. If you tell someone to write down their email so that you can let them know if they win a prize but then email them every week, they will feel lied to. Even if you did not specifically say there would be no extra emails, you lose credibility for not being upfront about it.

- If possible stay away from attachments. The client is more likely to read what is right in the text of the email as opposed to something they have to download first.

- Start and end your email with a warm salutation. You want to show your client that you care about them as soon as they open the email and remind them right before they close the email. Make sure the beginning and end of the email are friendly and personal.

- If the only reason you are emailing is to let them know something specific and you do not require a reply, let them know. It will make them even more likely to read the whole email knowing that there time won't be wasted trying to craft an answer at the end.

- Even if your email address is clear about who you are, announce it again in the email. Being specific about who the email is from will make them more comfortable. For example " This is John from (insert company here), I had a wonderful time talking to you yesterday and wanted to follow up..." Being transparent about the sender, especially if you have talked to the client in the past, is trustworthy. Even if it may seem obvious, because you just talked on the phone, you may want to reiterate who it is, in case they know another person with your name or something of that nature.

- Before sending your email, try reading it out loud. This way you will be sure you sound the way you want your client to hear you. Sometimes we write too formally or not formally enough without realizing it. Reading it out loud allows us to decide exactly what we want to sound like and perfect that tone in the email.

Email Marketing

- Pretend you are speaking to the reader in person. This will keep you from rambling in your email. Would you say everything that is written in your email if you were in front of them right now? This especially works for new clients or when you are trying to sell something. You would not walk up to someone and immediately start ranting about your product so don't do so in an email either. Sometimes if you think of your email as a text message, it will keep you from sending an email that is too long and drawn out. Text messages are always short and to the point because you don't have a full size keyboard and your small inconvenient keyboard makes you keep it brief. Just make sure you are still sending a professional email and not viewing it as if it was a text message to a friend, more like a text message to your employer.

- Complimenting your client is a good thing and a welcome part of your email but make sure the compliment is relevant and that it is not too long. A long drawn out compliment will make them feel as if you are trying to buy their trust with lies instead of coming off as the friendly compliment that your sister would give you. Compliments should be genuine. Only praise someone the way you would compliment your own family.

- If you received an email that was sent to multiple people, ask yourself whether they all require to see your response. You do not want to waste the time of anyone not relevant. Also, your reply may be more personal with information that you or the original sender would not want everyone to see. Never click "reply all" instead type out the name of every person you want to receive it, this way you never have any doubt that anyone unwanted or unneeded is receiving your email. After you have typed out the email, check again to make sure the person on the receiving end of the email is who you want it to be. Sometimes you can get distracted while writing an email and forget who it was originally to. If you take a break from writing your email to answer a call or speak to someone, make sure you reread the email in its entirety and who you are sending it to before continuing to type.

- When sending a one on one email personalize with comments that are strictly to the reader. For example mention their family, their hobby or something more professional like their office or website. Personalizing the email this way will let the client see that you know exactly who you are talking to and are obviously focused on them.

- Even when the sender is not necessarily waiting on a response or didn't specify that he needed one, send one anyway. It is important to let your clients know that you read and understand all their emails. There will also be no confusion later about whether you received the information that they were trying to get to you.

- Make sure your font size and type are easy to read and not brightly colored. Different computers will show the color slightly differently and you may end up giving your clients headaches by trying to have a colorful email. Also, you do not want the font to be too small or too large. A font that is too small can make it hard for some customers to read whereas a font that is too large looks unprofessional.

- Say thank you! Everyone likes being appreciated. If your client did something to make your life easier even in the smallest way, give him props for it. He didn't have to help you so make sure he knows you valued his initiative.

- Although questions are important for keeping the line of communication open, too many questions may do just the opposite. If they realize they will have respond to more than they feel they have time for, they will skip over your email. One or two questions are a great way to get a reply with frustrating the client.

- Do not forward any emails to clients unless it is specifically relevant to them. If you do decide to forward, make sure you add a note from yourself at the beginning. You need to make sure they know why the email was forwarded to them. Edit the forwarded email by making sure to delete unnecessary or personal content.

- Make sure the address you are sending emails from is appropriate and professional. If you have more than one email address, only use one for your client base and make sure it is the most professional one. An email address that only includes a version of your name and the email provider is most professional. Try not to have numbers or other letters and words if possible.

- Even though you know better than to forward an email, this is not true for everyone. When writing emails always imagine that your writing was forwarded to the worst possible person. Did you still come off as professional? Never say anything negative about any person. Talking about someone without their knowledge, even if you claim you are just telling facts, is inappropriate. Adding emotion to facts changes them to opinion. You can tell your client that John sent in their order on Tuesday but do not make comments such as "John finally sent in your order on Tuesday after I reminded him three times."

- Keep your emails as formal as possible until you know your client very well and know what he does or does not prefer when it comes to communication. The first few emails to new contacts should be very professional. Even though you are trying to make a lasting connection similar to a friendship, you must remember that you are selling yourself. You are catering to your clients and you cannot be sure what type of communication they prefer from you until you have had several emails back and forth.

- If an email has been going back and forth for a while, you can change the subject line to represent the actual discussion better. This will remind both you and your client about what the conversation is about when scanning your inbox.

- If you are bringing up a new topic to a client, do not reply to a previous email that is unrelated. Compose a brand new email. It is more professional and will not be confusing to the reader.

- Always add your new client emails to your contacts as soon as you receive them. You would not want their emails to accidentally end up in your spam folder. This is also a great way to keep your clients straight, You can add notes the contact and add any other information they have given you such as phone number or physical address. This will make it easy to follow up with them via phone or snail mail if they specifically ask.

- When clearing your spam and trash in your email, scan through so as to make sure you don't miss anything that is actually important and ended up there accidentally.

- If you are replying to a client's email and realize that you have felt disrespected in some way or frustrated by something they said, take a break before you respond to their email. You may even want to wait until morning before sending an answer. Sometimes sleep allows you to see things more clearly. You do not want to come off rude or unprofessional even if they did disrespect you. Remember to stay professional at all times despite the actions or words of your clients.

- Testimonials are a great way to build credibility. People love to hear that someone just like them used the product or had a good experience with the company. If possible, use a direct quote so that it comes off less as bragging and more as good business.

Every email is important. You are sending it for a reason so let your point get across in the best possible manner. Do not let yourself lose customers or email contacts because of simple things you could have, but did not do.

Chapter 7

Recurring Emails

What about recurring emails? What information might you have in a recurring email that you would not have in all the other emails? After all it is easy enough to get someone to read one email but will they really be interested in reading another one next week or next month? It is very common for someone to mark you as spam after several emails even if they specifically subscribed to your email list. You want them to stay interested in your emails and even anticipate them. Here are some tips on making sure they look forward to your email.

- Decide whether a recurring email is best for your company. Sometimes recurring emails are just a waste of time for both you and your clients. If you send bargain emails every once in a while and that does the trick then why hurt your confidence by trying to get a certain amount of people to open your email every single week? On the other hand if you are the type of business that needs to stay on their radar at all times then a recurring email might be exactly what you need. You are asking yourself "What type of business doesn't want to stay on the radar?" Good question. If you sell pool supplies, for example, you may not need to keep them up to date on what you have in stock every week. You may, however, want to send emails when coupons are available or if there are end of season sales. On the other hand if you are a dance studio or a gym, you have to email your students regularly to remind them of events. You also must remind them about coming to class and how much they love dance or about working out and their goals to stay in shape. Otherwise, if they stop attending and there are no emails to be sent, they may decide they are done and end their membership.

- Recurring emails are all about reminders. Since they are every single month or even every week, it is the perfect time to say "Hey, don't forget!" So if you have a sale or limited time offer coming up in October, why don't you remind them of it in both August and September so that they are really looking forward to it. Also, remind them of any events that are open to them. Get them excited about it months in advance so that they have written it on their calendar and are sure not to miss it.

- Checking your statistics on how many people opened your email or unsubscribed, can help you improve. When you have high open rates, remind yourself of what you did with that email and do it again. The opposite is important as well. If you had a lot of people unsubscribe right after a specific email, then try to decide what you may have done wrong. There is no teacher like experience. Make sure to learn from your mistakes as well as your triumphs.

- Decide what topics your monthly emails will include. Keep this consistent. The people who read your emails every month are doing so because they enjoy the content so keep them happy by continuing to write about the same topics. All the topics in your email must be related. A very diverse email may seem like a good idea but it is too chaotic and will not be conducive to people reading the whole email. Try to decide what is important to your emails and keep it consistent.

- Encourage feedback. Ask your subscribers if they found the email helpful. Ask them what their favorite article was in the past year. Ask them which section they dislike the most and why. Ask, ask, ask and then read the answers! Make it so that they can reply to your weekly newsletter or you can add an email address at the bottom that they can use to email their feedback. Either way take what they have to say to heart. These are your clients and they are more like each other than you may think. If you get a lot emails telling you they miss when you used to send them coupons every month then by all means, reinstate the coupons! If possible, reply to their feedback emails. Let them know you understand their concern or appreciate their tip. If you plan on following their advice, tell them. Let them know that you already have next month's emails written out but you will absolutely take their guidance to heart in the next set of emails. This way they are not feeling like you ignored their comment. Instead they are actually looking forward to those emails and feeling like they are a part of it. If for some reason you cannot or do not want to do what they proposed, consider telling them why. You can email them back for example and tell them "I really liked that part of my previous emails as well but I got an overwhelming amount of complaints about it so I decided to cut it out and do not think that adding it back in would be in the best interest of the newsletter at this point in time." Be polite and show that you really do care what they think even though you will not be performing the change as they requested. Always thank your clients for helping you by giving feedback. Customers love knowing that you listen to them. This makes you more credible because you are clearly putting them first and they can see it. Don't forget that making your clients happy is your number one priority.

- If you are sending emails every single week, take into account that certain days may be better than others to send them. If you are sending emails that include articles and topics to be read and enjoyed then Tuesday may be the best day. It has been researched and it seems that because people are more emotionally stressed on Tuesdays (from the very long work week ahead of them) they are more likely to open and read emails on this day. This may also be a good time to send a little motivation their way if that is something you plan on including in your email. On the other hand if you are specifically sending the email in order to push them to buy something or go somewhere, a "call to action" so to speak, you may want to send it later in the week. A Friday or Saturday is best since they then have all weekend to do shopping. They do not have the time for this during the week and may have already forgotten about it by the time the weekend comes around. These are also happier days and therefore they may feel more comfortable with the idea of spending money. Perhaps this is something that is relevant to your email, if you will be asking for them to purchase something or possibly donate to a cause.

- The other important research to keep in mind is the time of day to send your email. Although most may say morning is best, this may not be true especially during the week. It is correct to say that most people check and read their email first thing in the morning. The fact is, however, that during the work week people just had their coffee and are trying to get as much work done as possible first thing in the morning. This means that emails that are not from their own coworkers or business related may be put to the side for later and then forgotten about. If you are sending your email on a weekday, try sending it in the afternoon. The afternoon slump is a good time for clients to check their

Email Marketing

email. They may decide to read your email because they need a break from their own work and need to distract or clear their minds. On the other hand if you are sending your emails on Saturday, sending it in the afternoon may be a bad idea. Your "call to action" will be late since the weekend is halfway over by Saturday afternoon. This will cut in half your chances of them going to the store or purchasing your product.

- For a monthly newsletter you will want to follow the 90/10 rule. Since you are sending this email repeatedly, clients will get frustrated if they feel you are consistently pushing products and services on them. The 90/10 rule means that only 10% of your email should be focused on selling something. The other 90% should be content you know that your clients are interested in. This should be subject matter that uplifts them and motivates them. If most of your email is stimulating to them, the 10% that is selling will be more likely to succeed.

- If you are just sending the weekly newsletter in order to get more foot traffic to your website then consider sending a very short email. A short explanation of a new article or new product on your website with a picture and a link is just enough to get them to click and therefore end up on your website. This can be a very good idea if you don't have much to say every week. It will never be too much to look at and it gives your client the free reins to decide whether they want to follow the link without any pressure. Clients do not like pressure. This will definitely build your credibility. This is for only one kind of company however, so if you have news to tell or coupons to send out, opt out of this specific email tip. There is absolutely nothing wrong with the good old fashioned newsletter if that is what fits your clientele.

Email Marketing

- Keywords are a wonderful tool. The reason Google uses keywords to decide which order websites will be listed in, is because keywords tell the story of what the website is talking about. Subconsciously people look for these keywords as well. So even though you cannot look up your email newsletter on Google, you will still want to use keywords in both your subject line and actual email content. The way to find the best keywords for your topic is by researching the topic on Google, looking at the top few results and then reading the articles. Decide which words or phrases are used in all of the top websites. These will be the words you will want to incorporate into both your subject line and email content.

- Try to only have one promotion on your email. Yes, we talked about the 90/10 rule, but this is different. This is the part where you are telling someone go buy this or here is a coupon. Make sure in each recurring email you send, there is only one of these. More than one of these will make the reader unable to decide which to do or just turn them off of buying from you completely. If you have just one coupon or promotion then the buyer realizes right away what he must do. Surprisingly enough sometimes choices are overrated. This is like either having a to-do list or seeing a great offer. Which would you prefer? Make life easier for your customer by telling them exactly what they should do and keeping it simple. They will appreciate this.

- Use bold lettering. Bold letters will keep the email easy to read. If someone reads only the bold lettering, they will know which parts of your email they are interested in reading and which parts they can skip over.

- Leave enough space around your writing that is completely blank. When reading the email, you want your clientele to feel relaxed. If you squish everything together with lots of pictures and texts, the email will be more stressful than necessary. You will want to make sure that there is plenty of completely blank space around your writing that makes your email look shorter and easier to read.

- Construct your recurring email as if it was a story. The subject line is the introduction which gets the reader's attention. From there everything you write is leading up to the climax which for your company is probably whatever you are asking your client to do whether it be go shopping or donate to a nonprofit. Make the climax whatever is the most exciting part of your email though. These examples are just what the climax may be for certain companies. The conclusion of your story or email would be reinforcing your climax. Make your story exciting with the climax being the very best part.

- Try different things, including no images. Yes, images are great and enticing but for some companies they may be completely irrelevant and unimportant. If this seems like it may be the case for you, then try a no images email. If your email is well written and interesting, images may just get in the way.

- Plan your email schedule ahead of time. Decide what will be in each email for the year or month depending on how many you send at a time. Have your whole year or whole month planned out before you send out a single one. This will make your emails consistent and you are guaranteed not to run out of ideas because you already have them written down. This is a good time to also decide how often your email will be sent out. You must pick a timeline that will allow you to never run out of strong and interesting content. Also, take into consideration how much time you have to devote to writing these emails. No matter how important you feel a newsletter may be, a poorly written one will only hurt your credibility. Arrange a timetable that will work for you as well as stay interesting to your readers.

These tips should be a great starting point for all your different types of email marketing. They certainly do not each need to be followed to a tee. Pick which ones work for you and your company as well as your clientele. Do not forget that the most important thing is to keep your credibility as high as possible and this requires you to make sure all your email marketing content is based on you and your product as well as aimed at the correct group of people.

Chapter 8

Editing Your Email

You are not done after the initial typing of the email. You must now edit it. Grammatical and spelling errors hurt your credibility. Even though it is not a serious offense, every error adds to their suspicion of your character. It is hard for someone to feel safe buying or trusting a person that they feel is uneducated. If possible have someone else check it as well. Sometimes your eyes do not see the errors when you have been staring at the same words for quite a while.

Your spelling is not the only thing you should look for when editing your email. Here a few other things to check.

Make sure your emails looks like they came from you. You are the person that they gave their email address to and they will feel cheated if they think you had someone else write the email or you gave their information away. This is another place where your list of values and personality traits comes in handy. Even if you did write the email, it must sound like you. Make sure that your personality comes through the email. People love personality, not necessarily a certain personality but just the fact that they feel they are reading a person's work and not a robots.

Keep your email short. A long email is a big turn off. Time is precious. Keep your email to the point and interesting and most importantly short. When you are editing your email, cut down on as much information as possible. Remember they can always email you with questions but you will get no replies or questions if they never read it. Long emails are daunting and that is not what you are trying to be. If you do have a lot of information that you need to get out, try to have a clickable table of contents at the beginning so that clients can skip through to what is important and relevant to them.

The greeting is the first thing they will look at on your email. Try to keep it light and change it up every time. Do not simply say "Good Morning" every single email. Switch it up and make it interesting such as "Good Day Ladies and Gentlemen" or "Hello from (insert location here)". Whatever greeting you decide on, make sure to change it the next time around.

Care. Ask questions and put your client first. Of course they cannot answer as to how they are doing but they want to know that you want to know. Talk about things they want to hear about and make it clear that you are mentioning these things for them. Add an inspirational quote or a coupon. Tell them thank you for their subscription to your email list and mean it. All these things will make them feel like you wrote the email because you wanted them to receive it and read it and have a better day. You do not want them to think you sent the email so as to check it off your to-do list or add to your fan base.

Have a logo and add it to your emails. Not everyone has a logo but if possible you should have some type of defining factor for your company or product. A logo that stays the same for every email will make the customer feel at home in the email. If you are just designing your logo, think about keeping it simple. A simple logo will look better and clearer on email marketing. An uncomplicated, yet still unique logo is nicer to look at and looks better on a computer or cell phone.

Add blue if possible. For some reason the color blue brings about a feeling of safety and therefore trust. If you can incorporate the color blue into your logo or the background of the email, do so. This could be an easy way to increase your credibility.

If you use any statistics in your email, whether it be the number of products sold or a percentage of satisfied customers, use exact numbers. Do not use the phrase "almost 15000 copies sold". The exact number builds trust. An estimation hurts your credibility. It sounds like you are trying to make yourself sound better by rounding up. Your sales will not seem any less impressive with the exact number but you will seem more trustworthy.

Stick to your email schedule. If you have written out which emails will contain what content for the year, do not forget to follow your timetable. If you slightly deviate, it could mess up all of your plans for the month. If for some reason you feel that you have to deviate, rewrite your schedule entirely for that month forward. Consistency makes your clients feel more comfortable so articles that relate to each other are great tools. You look very prepared when, for example, all your articles in the month of October have to do with women, pink, or cancer. Write your email schedule before sending out any of your newsletters.

When editing your email, take into consideration that you may want to have questions in your content. When you ask all the different types of questions such as when, where, how, and why, you keep your reader focused. Decide whether you want to add any of these questions to make your content more interesting.

If you have any names of people in your email for example maybe in the testimonials, you will want to make sure they are spelled correctly. It is not a good feeling for a client to see his name in your article and realize you don't even know how to spell it. On the other hand if a client has a complicated name and sees that you spelled it correctly, they will think that you pay great attention to them and this is yet another thing that will add to your credibility.

If you have written about a topic that is outside the scope of your product or company, check to make sure all the details are correct. Research the topic just as well as you have researched your own product. If a client sees that your article is not based on facts, they will start to distrust you in all areas. Always check your facts.

If you would like use a website that allows you to pick a background for your newsletter. The pre-made designs are very easy to use and look great. If you would like to keep it simple and cheaper, there is nothing wrong with you writing a blank email, perhaps with a picture or two.

Have your deadline be a few days before the email is set to go out. The more cushion you give yourself to write and edit, the more likely you are to feel comfortable enough to send out the very best email you can.

Keep your language simple and easy to read. Even if most of your readers are very educated, a simple text will not hurt your credibility. It is easier for someone to read below their vocabulary than above. Write a simple yet interesting email.

If you have headlines or captions on your pictures, check all of them to make sure they are in the correct spot on your email.

If you have a portion of your email written by someone else, ask them to write a short "authors note." The writer will appreciate this and it will increase your credibility with your readers.

Remember that the writing in your email is more important than the way it looks. If possible, you want it all. You want it to look beautiful and read great but the first and most important thing is the content of your email. Make sure the content of your newsletter is interesting and well written before you worry about the background in the least bit.

If you have more than one article or section in your email, make sure the headlines are appropriate and interesting. Remember that the client does not have to read it, they can delete the email with one click. The headlines must call to them. When you open the email, do the headlines listed make you want to read the rest of the email? Make sure the most interesting headline is first. This is the one that will decide whether the person deletes the email or keeps reading.

Do not take the editing part of your email marketing lightly. Have multiple people review your email before you send it out and once that has been done look over it again yourself. Make sure you are the last person to see it before it is sent out. You do not want any of the changes from others to make the email feel like it is not from you. Do not forget how important it is to your credibility that you look prepared, educated, and caring.

Chapter 9

Your Subject Line

You have written your email and are about to send it but first you must add a subject line. A subject line can build or kill your short term credibility. This means that a person will either open or delete your email based on that subject line. A bad subject line is bad for the credibility of the sender. When you open your email and see a subject line that says "I was amazed by the results!" You automatically assume that it is junk mail. On the other hand a client who sees a so-so subject line might decide to leave it to read later. When this happens, chances are they will forget to read it altogether. This means that a good or great subject line is essential to get your reader to open your email in turn putting your company at the top of their mind.

So how do you come up with a great subject line? There are several ways to do this.

Keep your subject line short. Use it as if it was a title. Use as few words as necessary while still making sure to get your point across. It should definitely not go over seven words.

You can use pressing wordage such as "This week only." This will urge your reader to open as soon as possible to make sure they are not missing out on anything.

If you can hook the reader but keep them curious, you are golden. Give just enough information that they know they are interested but do not give away the punch line so that they are wondering what the climax of the email will be about.

A specific benefit that the reader may receive from reading your email such as specific information about something that is interesting to them can make a fine subject line. For example "Learn how to make delicious crepes."

When inviting your clients to an event, you can quote your call to action right in the subject line. For example "Join us for our 7th annual potluck."

Do not use all capitals or multiple punctuation marks. Also, try not to sound like a salesman in your subject line. No one wants to feel like they are being sold something even before they open the email. This is a sure way to have the email deleted.

Do not add dull unimportant words or numbers to your subject line. Every word in your subject line is precious. Use only the most interesting and relevant words. An example of extra unexciting words would be a subject line that read "Learn to make crepes with peanut butter and powdered sugar." You did not have to add the ingredients to the subject line. They will read the ingredient list soon enough. Instead have your subject line describe that these are the most delicious crepes they will ever taste instead. This is more exciting and interesting while keeping out boring words.

Prove to your reader that the content will be helpful as well as easily read by listing what they will learn in terms of numbers. For example "3 ways to..." or "...in 5 easy steps." These phrases will make the client feel that the email will be in a list format and that he will be able to open it, learn the details, and close it within minutes. The illusion of saving someone's time instead of wasting it is a great tool.

If an email is time sensitive, it may be helpful to send the email at a certain day or time that is relevant to the email. For example if kids eat free on Wednesday evenings, why not send the email on Wednesday around noon announcing "Wednesday is kid's day. They eat free!" If they are interested in this offer, they will open it immediately so that they can learn the details and take advantage of the offer right away.

If you have new and exciting news, you can list it right there in the subject line. The client will feel great knowing he is the first to find out.

Try not to use a do not reply email address. This is impersonal and keeps your clients at an arm's length. Do not forget you are trying to be as much of a friend as possible.

Adding an emoji to the subject line is very friendly and catches the eye. Do not use more than one but it can seem very personal to add just one. Make sure it matches the rest of your subject line.

Using a question as a subject line provokes curiosity. If they do not open the email after reading the question, they feel as if they left something unfinished.

If you are not sending a group email and therefore have a specific client in mind, adding their name to the subject line could increase the chance of them opening it. If their name is in the subject line then they will have no doubt that it is not just spam. On the other hand if it is an email to many clients, using the word "you" will still make it feel more one on one.

You have already made a list of who your target audience is. If you know what they want and who they care about then it is easy enough to just put exactly that in the subject line. An example of this would be if you work for an insurance company who is targeting older individuals for life insurance, you could put something such as "Your family's future" and make sure to add some topics about families in the email as well as your sales pitch.

Email Marketing

Mention something only your company can offer them, right in the subject line. For example "The chunkier our peanut butter, the better!" If you would like, you can even use the name of your product to reinforce that it is from you.

If you can offer a coupon or promotion for a specific city, list it in the subject line. Seeing the name of their own city in the subject line, makes it feel like it is more meant for them. You can also add in news from their location if you do not have a promotion for them. The idea is just to somehow include their location in the subject line.

A funny subject line is a great way to have someone open it. Everyone likes a little humor sometimes and they are not expecting it when going through their emails so the joke will be a nice and welcome change of pace.

Make your client feel significant right in the subject line. Compliment them or thank them but make sure they feel important.

If you can fit an interesting and relevant fact in your subject line, go for it. The reader will appreciate that he already learned something new and hasn't even opened the email yet proving that you are willing to impart information with nothing in return.

When you have a picture or video that hasn't been seen yet included in the email, tell them right in the subject line. Knowing there is something included that is new and exciting will get them to open it.

Another great subject line is one that makes a promise. It must be a promise that you can keep of course. If you, for example, promise a great coupon discount right on the subject line then your audience will open the email specifically to print out the coupon and in the process will see the rest of your email.

It is proven that numbers stop the eye when scanning your inbox which means if you can somehow work numbers into your subject line such as "4 great coupons" then it is more likely that the reader see it when he is quickly trying to sort through his inbox. You should not however add random numbers. Your credibility is at stake with everything you do. Putting random numbers in your subject line will make it a very weak subject line and hurt your trustworthiness. Your email will be noticed but also deleted.

The last tip for subject lines is actually not even about the phrase used. Friends open friend's emails which brings you back to making sure you are treating your clients like family. If a customer knows that he always gets something out of his emails from you, even if it is just the fact that they always make him smile, then he will look forward to opening it and do so as soon as he notices your name in the sender column. This will actually have nothing to do with the subject line and have everything to do with the connection between the two of you.

When writing your subject line, first and foremost decide whether you would open an email with that same subject line. Do not expect more from your clients than you would expect from yourself. Make your subject line interesting and relevant every single time.

Chapter 10

Selling in Your Email

If you are writing an email in order to sell something, do not forget your credibility is at stake. Certain things are essential to an email that is meant to be a pitch. You do not want to come off pushy or as if your only reason for contacting them is to sell. These things will hurt your reputation because they will assume you do not care for them. Don't forget that you are emailing as a friend.

Be a friend first, before pitching anything, make sure you mention some things to make them feel comfortable reading. Make them really feel as if they have just opened an email from a friend. For example:

"Hi John,

I was just thinking the other day how thankful I am to have you as a customer and friend. The business I do would just not be the same without you..."

This example is very vague but you can make it your own based on what you are trying to sell and who your clientele is.

Next, make sure you mention some great things about your product. Bringing down the competition is the opposite of what you are aiming for. You want to keep their thoughts positive, therefore you mention the fact that "25% of the proceeds is going to be donated to homeless shelters" or mention the "Freshly baked cookies scent" that your product will add to their home. These are the reasons why they are buying your product so make sure they match your target audience and what is important to them.

Do not forget that the client can email you back asking questions and you can go back and forth quite a few times relaying information. This means that there is no reason you have to cram everything about your product into one email and make the client feel attacked with information. You have to assume that the first email will not seal the deal. A connection with the client must be made over several emails. Your first sales email should just be enough to get the client interested enough to contact you.

When you are describing your product, believe in it and make sure you make it sounds as valuable to your client as possible. The reason you are selling it is because it is valuable so do not sell yourself or your product short. Make it sound just as great as it really is.

Adding your opinion to the sales email is actually a good thing. Be as respectful as possible but people will welcome the honesty and will feel you are a more trustworthy salesman as well. Even if the opinion is not well-liked and especially if it is not popular. This will still build rapport. They will see that you are being completely and unapologetically yourself and admire it. Surprisingly, opinions are a great sales technique.

Bribe them into buying your product by offering more than expected. Provide an additional thank you gift added to their package. Offering motivation for them to share your product or service with their friends is also a great way to add on more sales.

Using references to famous people such as jokes or quotes will keep the tone enjoyable and make a connection. They will realize that they are fond of the same television shows and books as you are, creating a relationship between the two of you.

Make them not want to miss out. You want them to feel as if they will be losing something if they do not take the bait. Mention all the great advantages your product offers that they will have to miss out on completely without purchasing it.

Tell a story. This will help keep your sales pitch light. It will help them feel less like a client and more like a friend. Make sure it relates of course, but a good story will keep them interested in your email, in you, and in your product.

The sooner they buy it, the better it is for you. Even if they completely plan on purchasing your product, if they procrastinate, chances are they will forget. Give them a reason to buy it now. A special price is always an easy way to do this but there are other ways as well. For example you could offer it to only a certain amount of people. That will get them to do it as fast as possible because they do not know how fast others may snatch it up.

Telling the client how to purchase it or sign up is very important. Even if it seems to be quite easy, sometimes you may not realize that someone is reading this email first thing in the morning when they are tired and impatient or last thing before bed when they are just ready to go to sleep. You must have clear instructions in your email on how to buy the product. This will make it easy for them no matter what time it is or how clear their head might be.

The very last thing you need in order to sell the product is a PS. Yes, those last little words before they close the email are very important. These are the last words they see so make them count. You can take this opportunity to remind them that the offer is only for a limited time therefore making them go back into the email to actually purchase it. You could also use this opportunity to remind them that you are a friend and they can trust you, such as "I really appreciate you reading this email, I know that you are busy and hope you are doing well." This will help build your credibility with them. They will appreciate the fact that the last thing on your mind is them and not your product.

Chapter 11

Ways to Get Email Addresses

You are selling your product and need to as well as want to market this commodity via email. Your question is how will you convince any clients to give you their email addresses? There are a number of ways you can do this.

- Social Media- Your fans on Facebook and followers on twitter are good candidates for your email list. They clearly already enjoy your posts so now all you have to do is persuade them that signing up for your email list will be an extra benefit. One way you could do this would be to sometimes post an excerpt of your email on your social media. When you do this, post a link to signing up for the email list and make it clear that the rest of the article is in your newsletter.

- Website- Have a very clear link to your email list on your website. If your customers do not know how to sign up for the email list, this could be a very big problem. Also, try not to have it be as simple as a "sign up for our emails here." Add something to the link that specifically says why they are signing up such as "sign up for our weekly coupons and emails!"

- Sharing- Ask your current subscribers to tell their friends. If they truly enjoy the content and the perks of your email, they should want to share it. One way to make it easier for them is by having a button they can press to share some of the email content either on their own social media accounts or with a specific friend they have in mind.

- Raffle- You can earn email addresses through a raffle. It is extremely important to tell your clientele that they are signing up for the email list when entering the raffle. They probably won't have an issue with this though since they are so excited about the prospect of winning a prize.

- Incentive- A weekly coupon or article that cannot be found elsewhere are incentives for them to want to sign up. The only way to get the coupon or the other content is to join the email list. This will make them feel appreciated as if they were a VIP.

- Physical Locations- Post a sign up list in physical locations that your clientele like to meander. With a great well-written flyer, you should be able to get a few good email addresses.

Do not let a lack of email addresses hurt your email marketing. You have put so much work into planning and writing your emails, make sure you have a number of subscribers that can enjoy your hard labor.

Chapter 12- Building Your Credibility Some More

Other things that will build your credibility are the things you do every day and the person you are day in and day out. Earning credibility may seem like a slow process sometimes but it is completely worth it. If a client loves and trusts you that is when they will feel comfortable telling their friends about you and therefore growing your company. Believe it or not your humility and respect for others will come through an email and the lack thereof will as well. Respect of others is extremely important. Respect is a two way street and you will not receive respect without giving it. In your conversations with others as well as your emails and online marketing, make sure to be professional in all things. Stay respectful of others even when they are not respectful of you. Being able to stay calm in all situations makes you look professional and builds credibility. If you argue with a client, this news will spread like wildfire and your trustworthiness will very quickly diminish. It may be hard to be respectful when being insulted but it is of the utmost importance. When someone complains to you, listen to understand. Did you make a mistake? If yes, own up to it and fix it. Mistakes do happen. A mistake will not kill your credibility but lying about it will.

Always do the right thing. Do not cross the lines that you have set for yourself. An unwavering loyalty to yourself and your beliefs is credible. Breaking your own rules is not.

If you do not know how to answer a question, do not lie or make up an answer. Be honest with your client and yourself. Tell them that you are not sure what the answer is but you will find out and let them know as soon as possible. They will appreciate your honesty more than an inappropriate answer.

You need to realize that some people will not like you. It is impossible for someone to please everyone. Accept this fact and move on. There are plenty of people out there, you do not need to keep trying to satisfy someone who cannot be satisfied. You must be respectful about it though, your integrity is on the line even with those who do not like you. Word of mouth is a very strong tool and someone who has had a bad experience with you will spread this news whereas someone who just did not agree with you will have no problem continuing with their day. Be respectful and move on.

At first glance it may seem that credibility does not have much influence on email marketing and the other way around. This, however, is incorrect. Your email marketing will succeed only if your client believes you are a credible source. On the other hand, your reputation can either be tarnished or polished by the way you market your product. Email marketing is a highly effective tool when it is used correctly by a salesperson with integrity and trustworthiness.

Conclusion

Thank you again for purchasing this book!

I hope this book was able to help you to market your ideas, products, and services while increasing your credibility. Credibility is not black and white it is something that grows or diminishes depending on your actions. Your credibility will impact how the customer feels about you and therefore whether he buys from you. This book has given you very specific tips on what you should or should not do in specific situations in order to ensure it only grows and your clients trust you more and more with every encounter.

You have made a smart decision when opting to market your product through email. Even with social media being so prevalent these days, email marketing is still one of the smartest ways to get your company name out there. It is an easy way to target an audience or several audiences and sell to them the specific products they might be interested in. You are able to do this without wasting any of their time or your own. It even allows you to personalize the emails if you would like and best part is, they receive it the moment you send it.

The next step is to start off writing down everything you know about yourself and your product. Don't forget that this is a very important step. It will allow your clients to have confidence in you and grow your connection with them.

Once you've done this you can move on to making an email list and writing your email. Make sure you follow the tips throughout the whole process to make everything easier while also building trust with your clients.

To grab your copy of both of the Ebooks.

Visit www.mrmarketinghero.com/freebook

Below I would like to know your opinion of my book, let me know what you think.

Finally, if you enjoyed this book, then I'd like to ask you for a favor, would you be kind enough to leave a review for this book on Amazon? It'd be greatly appreciated!

Thank you and good luck!